Eyewitness

FOOTBALL

DON DU **PÉTROLE HAHN** POUR LES CHEVEUX

GRAND MATCH D'ASSOCIATION

1930s French hair oil
advertisement

1930s painting
of a goalkeeper

1900s football pumps

1900s
shin-pads

1910s
shin-pads

1930s
shin-pads

Early
20th-century
football
stencils

Steven Pienaar
of South
Africa

1966 World
Cup football

1998 World Cup football

1905 match
holder

Early
20th-century
porcelain
figure

Early
20th-century
porcelain
figure

Eyewitness
FOOTBALL

Written by
HUGH HORNBY

Photographed by
ANDY CRAWFORD

1912 football

in association with
THE NATIONAL FOOTBALL MUSEUM

19th-century jersey

1925 Australian International shirt

1905 book cover image

Early 20th-century snap card

THE REFEREE

LONDON, NEW YORK,
MELBOURNE, MUNICH, and DELHI

Project editor Louise Pritchard
Art editor Jill Plank
Assistant editor Annabel Blackledge
Assistant art editor Yolanda Belton
Managing art editor Sue Grabham
Senior managing art editor Julia Harris
Production Kate Oliver
Picture research Amanda Russell
DTP designers Andrew O'Brien and Georgia Bryer

THIS EDITION
Consultant Ed Wilson
Editors Ashwin Khurana, Surbhi Nayyar Kapoor
Designers Deep Shikha Walia, Honlung Zach
Picture researcher Sumedha Chopra
Managing editor Gareth Jones
Managing art editor Philip Letsu
Publisher Andrew Macintyre
Pre-production producer Adam Stoneham
Senior Producer Charlotte Cade

Publishing Director Jonathan Metcalf
Associate Publishing Director Liz Wheeler
Art Director Phil Ormerod

Jacket editor Rashmi Rajan
Jacket designer Govind Mittal

This Eyewitness ® Guide has been conceived by
Dorling Kindersley Limited and Editions Gallimard

First published in Great Britain in 2000
This revised edition published in Great Britain in 2014
by Dorling Kindersley Limited, 80 Strand, London WC2 0RL

Copyright © 2000, © 2004, © 2010, © 2014
Dorling Kindersley Limited
A Penguin Random House Company

Text copyright © 2000, © 2004 The National Football Museum

2 4 6 8 10 9 7 5 3
006 - 256697 - 03/14

A CIP catalogue record for this book is
available from the British Library.

ISBN: 978-1-4093-4936-5

Colour reproduction by Colourscan,
Singapore, and MDP, UK
Printed and bound by
South China Printing, China

Discover more at
www.dk.com

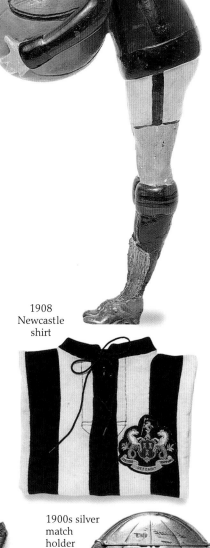

1900s plaster figure

1908 Newcastle shirt

1900s silver match holder

1930s silver hatpin

1920s silver flint lighter

Shirts from 1890s catalogue

Contents

Hungary badge Holland badge Italy badge Brazil badge

Early 20th-century child's rattle

1930s child's painted rattle

The global game

FOOTBALL HAS ITS ROOTS IN ancient China, Europe, and the Americas. People kicked a ball to prepare for war, to honour their gods, or just to entertain themselves. For centuries, different versions of ball-kicking games existed. In Europe, they were tests of courage and strength and in China and other eastern countries, the games were rituals of grace and skill. The rules of the modern game of football were not drawn up until 1863, but the qualities that we admire in it – speed, agility, bravery, and spirit – have been present in many cultures for more than 2,000 years.

An Ashbourne ball

ASHBOURNE BALL
Ashbourne in Derbyshire, England, is the site of one of several traditional Shrove Tuesday football games. It is characterized by disorder. Two teams, the Upwards and the Downwards, try to move the ball through the opposition's "goal" – a gateway at the other end of town.

HARROW BALL
English public schools, including Harrow and Eton, played a crucial role in developing modern football in the early 1800s. Although each school played the game differently, they all produced detailed, written rules. These provided the basis for the first official laws.

The Harrow ball was flattened, top and bottom, to allow it to skim across muddy playing fields

FOOTBALL TRAINING
The Chinese were playing a type of football by the 3rd century BCE. A military book of that period refers to *tsu chu*, or "kicking a ball". The game may once have been part of a soldier's training and was later included in ceremonies on the emperor's birthday.

足球

Chinese characters meaning "football"

A GENTLEMEN'S GAME
The game of calcio was played in Italian cities such as Venice and Florence in the 16th and 17th centuries. On certain festival days, two teams of gentlemen would attempt to force the ball through openings at either end of a city square. Although physical contact was a feature of calcio, the game also had a tactical element. Teams used formations and attempted to create space in which to advance.

Local people came out to watch the games

Handling the ball was part of the game

Players have to wear an elaborate costume of silk and gold brocade

Ball made from strips of leather

Men from many different backgrounds played football

STREET GAMES
This early 19th-century cartoon is subtitled "Dustmen, coalmen, gentlemen, and city clerks at murderous if democratic play". It shows the violent "every man for himself" spirit common to street games in Britain at that time. The damage done to property, particularly windows, and the disruption to the lives of other citizens caused many town councils to ban football – without much success.

ANCIENT RITUAL
The Japanese game of kemari probably developed in the 7th century from an ancient Chinese football game, after contact was made between the two countries. In contrast to the chaotic early football brawls of Europe, it involved many rituals and was played as part of a ceremony. The game is still played today and involves keeping the ball in the air inside a small court.

Kemari is a game of balance and skill

FOOTBALL WRITING
Football has been a popular literary subject for as long as the game has been played. The first-known book devoted to football is *Discourse on Calcio* by Giovanni da Bardi, published in 1580 in Florence, Italy. Football has inspired poetry too. "A Match at Football" by Matthew Concanen was published in an anthology in the 18th century. The popularity of football increased rapidly in the early 20th century. *The School Across the Road* by Desmond Coke is one of many children's books published at around that time.

16th-century discourse on football

18th-century anthology

The children's book *The School Across the Road*

Colour plates appear throughout the book

Image from a 9th-century watercolour on silk

History of football

THE GAME THAT HAS CAPTURED the imagination of people all over the world was developed in England and Scotland in the 19th century. The former pupils of English public schools produced the first common set of rules and formed the Football Association (FA) in 1863. Things moved forwards quickly. British administrators, merchants, and engineers took the game overseas and people from other countries began to play football. The first international matches were followed by professional leagues and big competitions.

CELEBRITY PLAYER
The first footballers were amateurs. C B Fry, who played for the Corinthians in the late 1890s, was one of the first football celebrities. He was also a member of the England cricket team and held the world long-jump record.

Arnold Kirke Smith's cap

EXHIBITIONISM
Throughout the early years of the 20th century, British teams toured the world, introducing football to other countries by playing exhibition matches. This shield was presented to the Islington Corinthians in Japan, in 1937.

Kinnaird once did a headstand after winning a Cup final

The English Three Lions motif was first used in 1872

Arnold Kirke Smith's England shirt

The shirt is made of closely woven wool

THE FIRST INTERNATIONAL
In November 1872, Scotland played England on a cricket field in Glasgow in the first ever international match. About 2,000 spectators watched a 0–0 draw. This shirt and cap were worn by Arnold Kirke Smith from Oxford University, who was a member of the English team.

MODERN RULES
Lord Kinnaird was president of the Football Association from 1890–1923, and was one of the amateurs who shaped the rules and structure of the modern game. He played in nine of the first 12 FA Cup finals, winning five.

TALENTED TEAMS
The English Football League began in 1888. Its 12-team fixture programme was inspired by US baseball. This 1893 painting by Thomas Hemy shows two successful clubs of the 1890s: Aston Villa who won the league five times and Sunderland, "the team of all talents", who won three times.

THE UNRULY GAME
The first French football league, set up in 1894, was dominated by teams of Scottish emigrants, such as the White Rovers and Standard AC. French satirists were quick to refer to the game's reputation for unruliness. This 1900s French magazine, *Le Monde Comique*, reflects this attitude towards the game.

In reality, women's kit was far less figure-hugging

A ball of exaggerated size

Bystanders often got caught up in the boisterous action

Cover illustration entitled *"Les Plaisirs du Dimanche"* ("Sunday Pleasures")

LADIES FIRST
Women's football started at the end of the 19th century. Teams such as the British Ladies Club attracted large crowds. During World War I, men's and women's teams played against each other for charity. The first women's World Cup was held in China in 1991 and was won by the USA.

FIFA badge

FORMING FIFA
By 1904, several countries, including France, Belgium, Denmark, the Netherlands, Spain, Sweden, and Switzerland had their own administrators. They formed the world governing body, FIFA (Fédération Internationale de Football Associations). By 1939, more than 50 countries had joined.

This 1900s plaster figure is wearing shin-pads that were typical of that time

Ugandan batik

Each stamp shows a different US player

US stamps produced for the 1994 World Cup

OUT OF AFRICA
Football spread through Africa from both ends of the continent. South Africa, with its European populations, was an obvious foothold and sent a touring party to South America in 1906. In 1923, Egypt became the first African team to join FIFA. In 2010 South Africa became the first African country to host the World Cup finals.

SOCCER
Soccer is one of the most popular youth sports in the USA, for both boys and girls. The 1994 World Cup Finals held in the USA provided a big boost for Major League Soccer, which is bringing top-level professional games to a new audience.

Laws of the game

THE RULES OF A GAME should be brief and easy to understand. It is certain that football's success has been due partly to the simplicity of its Laws. Rules governing equipment, the pitch, foul play, and restarts have all survived the passage of time. Football has always been a free-flowing game. Stoppages can be avoided if the referee uses the advantage rule – allowing play to continue after a foul, providing that the right team still has the ball. The offside rule has always been a source of controversy in the game. The assistant referees must make split-second decisions about whether an attacker has strayed beyond the second last defender at the moment the ball is played forwards by one of his or her team-mates. A player cannot be offside from a throw-in.

STAND BACK
This throw-in is illegal. The ball is held correctly in both hands but the feet, though they are both on the ground as they should be, are over the line.

There have been goal posts since the early days of football but, until the crossbar was introduced in 1875, tape was stretched between them 2.5 m (8 ft) from the ground

The penalty spot is 12 yd (11 m) from the goal-line

Goal kicks must be taken from within the 6-yd (5.5-m) box

Players must not cross the halfway line until the ball is kicked off

PENALTY
Penalties were introduced in 1891 as a punishment for foul play, such as tripping, pushing, or handball within 12 yd (11 m) of the goal. A player shoots at goal from the penalty spot with only the goalkeeper to beat. If the ball rebounds from the post or bar the penalty taker cannot play it again before someone else has touched it.

FREE KICK
There are two types of free kick – direct and indirect. In an indirect free kick, awarded after an infringement of a Law, the ball must be touched by two players before a goal is scored. Direct free kicks are given after fouls and the taker may score immediately. Opposing players must be at least 10 yd (9 m) away from the ball at a free kick.

CORNER
A corner kick is taken when the defending team puts the ball out of play behind their own goal-line. Corner kicks provide useful goal-scoring opportunities. The ball must be placed within the quadrant – a quarter circle with a radius of 1 yd (1 m) in the corner of the pitch. A goal can be scored directly from a corner kick.

FAKING FOULS
The amateur footballers of the 19th century believed that all fouls were accidental and would have been horrified by the "professional foul", an offence deliberately committed to prevent an attack from developing. Unfortunately, the game today is full of deliberate fouls. Some players also fake being fouled to win their team a free kick.

When a penalty is taken, only the taker is allowed inside the "D"

CHARGE!
The 1958 English FA Cup final between Manchester United and Bolton Wanderers is remembered for the disputed goal scored by Bolton's centre-forward, Nat Lofthouse. He charged the United goalkeeper, Harry Gregg, over the line as he caught the ball – a challenge that all referees today would consider a foul.

Players from the defending team must stay out of the 10-yd (9-m) circle before the kick-off

Players cannot be offside in their own half of the pitch

The 6-yd (5.5-m) box was semi-circular until 1902. The penalty box was introduced in the same year

Assistant referees patrol opposite sides of the field and cover one half each, their main responsibilities being to signal throw-ins and flag for offside

LAW AND ORDER
There are 17 main football Laws. The field of play must be rectangular and, for a full-size pitch, from 110 to 120 yd (100.5 to 110 m) long and from 70 to 80 yd (64 to 73 m) wide. There should be 11 players per side. Substitution rules have changed over the years and teams may now substitute any three from five players, including the goalie, during stoppages in the match. The duration of play is 90 minutes, in two halves of 45 minutes each.

PERMANENT MARKERS
In the mid-19th century, before it was stipulated that permanent lines should be marked on the pitch, flags were used as a guide to whether the ball was out of play. Today, a corner flag has to be at least 1.5 m (5 ft) high to avoid the risk of players being impaled.

Goal nets, patented by Brodies of Liverpool, England, in 1891, were first officially used in 1892 and were welcomed as a means of settling disputes over whether a ball had actually entered the goal

The referee

Early 20th-century snap card caricature of a referee

Eᴀʀʟʏ ᴀᴍᴀᴛᴇᴜʀ players put a high value on fair play but saw the need for officials on the football pitch. To begin with, each team provided an umpire from their own club, who did not interfere much with the passage of play. At this stage, players had to raise an arm and appeal for a decision if they felt that they had been fouled, otherwise play continued. The rise of professional football in the 1880s made it harder for umpires to be neutral. A referee was introduced to settle disputes. In 1891, the referee was moved onto the field of play and the umpires became linesmen, a system that has continued ever since. Linesmen and women are now called assistant referees.

YOUR NUMBER'S UP
One duty of the assistant referee is to control the entrance of substitutes to the field and check their boot studs. At top levels of the game, a fourth official uses an illuminated board to indicate the shirt number of the substitute and the player being replaced, and also inform everyone how much stoppage time will be played at the end of each half.

CLASSIC BLACK
This is the classic referee's uniform, all-black with white cuffs and collar. Dating from the 1970s, this kit is similar to all those worn after the phasing out of the blazer in the 1940s to the introduction of other colours in the 1990s. The bulky jackets of the early 1900s were replaced by a less constricting shirt to encourage the officials to keep up with play on the pitch.

White trim sets off the all-black kit

Notebook to record bookings, goals, sendings-off, and substitutions

The yellow card is shown for bookable offences

Serious foul play results in a red card and a sending-off

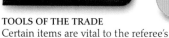

1940s Acme whistle

Both sides of a FIFA Fair Play coin

Badge refers to the referee's local association

Referees must be smartly turned out, with shirt tucked in at all times

Referees may carry a handkerchief in case players get dirt in their eyes

TOOLS OF THE TRADE
Certain items are vital to the referee's job. Red and yellow cards may seem like a long-established part of football but they were introduced only in the 1970s. It is believed the whistle was first used in 1878 and it was soon recognized as the best way of controlling play. Barrel-shaped whistles used to predominate but other shapes are now common. The referee carries a notebook and pencil to record details of the match and a special coin that is tossed to decide which team kicks off and in which direction.

YOU'RE BOOKED

Bookings used to be given only once or twice per match and sendings-off were extremely rare, but FIFA now insist that referees are much stricter. As a result, teams regularly have to play with 10 team members, or even fewer.

A red card is shown when a player has committed two bookable offences

A whistle is blown to indicate the start or restart of play, or to stop play due to a foul or injury

Former USSR

Australia

New Zealand

Bangladesh

Iceland

Portugal

USA

Colombia

Italy

WORLD-CLASS REFEREES

These badges are produced by Referees' Associations around the world. Despite all the abuse they receive, referees are motivated by the prospect of officiating at top-class games. World Cup matches are controlled by officials from all countries affiliated to FIFA, not just those that qualify as competitors.

LINESMAN FIFA 92   LINESWOMAN FIFA 95

Official FIFA badges for sewing on the officials' shirts

Men and women officiate at top-level football matches

TOUCHLINE HELPERS

The first linesmen waved a handkerchief to alert the referee. Assistant referees today use a flag. They wave the flag when a player is off-side, when the ball is out of play, and when they have seen an infringement on the pitch.

Referees have to be fit to keep up with play on the pitch

The first referees wore plus-two trousers

Blazer with pockets for a stopwatch and notebook

HOW TO BE A REFEREE

This illustration from the cover of a 1906 book entitled *How to be a Referee* shows the typical referee's clothing of that period. After taking a qualifying exam, referees usually start out at amateur level. They are assessed regularly to ensure that standards remain high. Today's top referees are professional. They earn good salaries for officiating top games.

The pitch

This Samuel Brandão painting shows football being played on bare earth in Rio de Janeiro, Brazil

Patterns can be made when mowing the pitch

At THE START OF A SEASON, footballers can look forward to playing their first match on a smooth green pitch. If a pitch is not looked after, it soon becomes muddy and uneven, especially if cold, wet weather sets in. Ground staff try to keep the pitches in good condition with the help of new species of grass and good drainage. In many northern European countries, football takes a midwinter break during the worst conditions. Wealthy clubs may lay a completely new pitch between matches, but millions of amateur players have to make do with whatever muddy or frozen land is available.

STREETS AHEAD

In the days before traffic became too heavy, street football was a popular pastime. Children learned close ball control and dribbling skills in confined spaces. They often used heaps of clothes or gateways as goalposts.

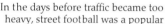

Jean-Pierre Papin playing for AC Milan, Italy, on a snow-covered pitch

Ground staff preparing for a match during the 1953 English season

PLAYING IN SNOW

In snowy weather, the pitch markings and the white football are hard to see and the ground is slippery. If the markings can be swept clear and the pitch is soft enough to take a stud, play can usually carry on, using a more visible orange ball.

HOT STUFF

In countries where the weather is cold during the football season, many methods have been tried to prevent pitches from freezing. Undersoil heating was first installed in England at Everton in 1958. Before undersoil heating became common, ground staff put straw down as insulation and lit fires in braziers to lift the air temperature. Today, large covers are sometimes used to protect pitches.

SLOPES AND SHADE

Modern pitches, such as Brighton and Hove Albion's *(above)*, are usually laid with a camber, which means that they slope slightly down from the centre circle to the touchlines. This helps to drain water away. When large stands are built, less air and light reach the grass, stunting its growth. This has been a problem at some stadiums, such as the San Siro in Milan, Italy.

PAMPERING THE PITCH

Modern pitch maintenance is a full-time job. In the summer, the grass must be mowed, watered, and fed regularly. During the close season, work is done to repair holes and worn patches in the turf. New types of grass have been developed that grow better in the shade of tall stands. This is vital in helping the ground staff to keep the pitch in good condition.

The surface is made to mimic grass

Fibres are woven together to form a carpet

Artificial grass viewed from the side, top, and underneath

Grass is kept long to encourage deep rooting

Layer of topsoil nourishes the grass

Heating pipes laid in grids

Layers of sand and gravel allow water to filter away

The base of the pitch is composed of large pieces of stone

Drainage pipes carry away water

Model of a section through a pitch

BETTER THAN THE REAL THING?

Artificial pitches are made from synthetic turf laid on a shock-absorbent pad. They are more hard-wearing than grass pitches and are unaffected by torrential rain or freezing cold. Clubs with an artificial pitch can rent out their stadium for a range of events, such as pop concerts, and their home matches need never be postponed because of bad weather. Many players do not like the surface because they feel that it increases the risk of injury.

SATURATION POINT

Rainwater is the greatest threat to pitch condition. Good built-in drainage is therefore an important part of pitch construction. Pipes and materials chosen for their good draining qualities are laid under the grass. A large amount of sand is mixed into the topsoil to make it less absorbent and less prone to becoming waterlogged. Even a well-cared-for pitch may become saturated. Ground staff sometimes have to resort to using garden forks to remove standing water.

Football skills

Early 20th-century button showing a man heading the ball

Eᴀᴄʜ ᴘᴏsɪᴛɪᴏɴ ᴏɴ ᴛʜᴇ ꜰɪᴇʟᴅ is associated with a specific range of tasks. Defenders must be able to tackle the opposition and claim the ball, midfielders need to pass the ball accurately to their team-mates, and strikers have to shoot and score goals. Although most players specialize in a certain position, professional players are expected to master a range of skills and work on any weaknesses. As part of their daily training routine, they practise hard to perfect their skills so that their technique does not let them down in a match.

CONTROL FREAK
The best players, like England's Wayne Rooney, can always bring the ball under control. To deal with high passes, players need to keep their eye on the ball and use their chest, stomach, head or, like Rooney here, their thighs to stun the ball.

Players call out to each other to indicate their intentions on the ball

TACKLE TALK
Players try to take the ball from another player by tackling. Germany's Mats Hummels is one of the finest tacklers in modern football. He shows the anticipation and timing that are essential to avoid committing a foul. Referees punish players if they make a physical challenge from behind or if they make contact with a player instead of the ball.

PASS MARK
Moving the ball quickly around the pitch, from one player to another, is the most effective means of stretching a defence. Accurate passing remains the hallmark of all successful teams. Barcelona's star passer of the ball is Xavi. He has the vision to pass the ball into space for his strikers even when he is tightly marked.

Constant movement into space is essential

If the defender is unable to reach the ball, he must still challenge the striker

All parts of the foot are used to manipulate the ball in the desired direction

The ability to pass with both feet gives the player more options

The player must time his leap to meet the ball firmly

HEADS UP!
There are two distinct kinds of heading, defensive and attacking. Defenders try to gain distance when they clear a high ball out of the goal area. Attackers need accuracy and power to score goals with a header. Ivory Coast striker Didier Drogba uses his height to beat the opposition and head the ball into the net.

Keeping the head still improves accuracy

WINGING IT

Crosses, or passes in from the wings, result in more goals than any other angle of attack. Players who can put the ball over with pace and accuracy are extremely valuable to a team. Portugal and Real Madrid winger Cristiano Ronaldo arguably takes the world's greatest free kicks. He is able to put great power behind the ball while also applying curve or dip. He plants his left foot firmly alongside the ball and uses his arms to maintain balance before driving his right foot through the ball. The way his foot strikes the ball dictates the dip or curl required.

The player can pretend to go in one direction before going in the other

DOWNTOWN DRIBBLER

When a player runs with the ball at his feet, it is called dribbling. Brazilian star Ronaldinho, who learned his football on the streets of Porto Alegre, is proof that dribbling can cause problems for the opposition. Good balance and concentration help a dribbler to change direction quickly and ride tackles.

Extending the arms assists with balance

Keeping body weight over the ball makes it easier to cross with power

The foot turns in as it passes through the ball to make it swerve

Keeping your head down and looking at the ball rather than the goal helps to ensure clean contact

The bicycle kick is even harder if the ball is moving across the player

GOING FOR GOAL

When shooting, forwards need the accuracy to find the corner of the net as well as the power to blast the ball through the defence. Edinson Cavani of Uruguay is one of the most reliable goalscorers in world football.

The left leg is firmly planted to allow the body to make the best shape for the cross

BICYCLE KICK

The bicycle kick was first demonstrated in the 1930s by Brazilian forward Leonidas. It is one of the most difficult skills to pull off. With their back to the goal, strikers throw their legs up in the air and kick the ball while falling backwards. This tactic sometimes catches the goalkeeper by surprise. This model of Italian striker Roberto Baggio shows the ideal body position.

A higher jump allows the player to keep the ball down below the crossbar

A 1900s match holder showing a goalkeeper punching clear

The goalkeeper

As the last line of defence, a goalkeeper knows that a single mistake can cost the team victory. Goalkeeping can be a lonely job. It entails having different skills from the rest of the team and you can be unoccupied for several minutes at a time. The recent change to the back-pass law, forcing the goalkeeper to kick clear rather than pick up the ball, has made the job even harder. The necessity of having both a physical presence and great agility means that goalkeepers have to train as hard as any other player, but the reward for this diligence can be a much longer career than that of their team-mates.

Clothes

Until 1909, goalkeepers were distinguishable only by their cap, making it difficult for the referee to judge who, in a goalmouth scramble, was handling the ball. From 1909 to the early 1990s, they wore a shirt of a single plain colour that was different from the shirts worn by the rest of their team. A rule was made forbidding short sleeves which has now been relaxed.

GOOD SAVE
This 1950 comic cover shows the save that is considered to be the easiest to make – from a shot straight to the midriff. It also hints at the spectacular action in which goalkeepers are regularly involved, such as when they have to fly through the air to tip the ball away. Modern strikers are likely to make the ball swerve suddenly, so it is all the more important for goalies to keep their bodies in line with the ball.

CATCH IT
Punching the ball away from the danger area has always been popular among European and South American goalkeepers. The goalkeeper depicted on this 1900 book cover is trying to punch the ball but he probably should be trying to catch it because he is not being closely challenged. In the modern game, referees rarely allow goalkeepers to be charged when they are attempting to catch the ball.

The ball should be punched out towards the wing

KEEPERS' COLOURS
Patterns in football shirts have traditionally been limited to stripes and hoops, but since the rules on goalkeepers' clothes were relaxed, every combination of colours seems to have been tried. Not all of them have been easy on the eye, although fluorescent designs are easy for defenders to see.

Flexible plastic ribs reinforce each finger

Modern gloves help to prevent injuries such as a broken finger

The shamrock, symbol of Ireland

EIRE SHIRT
This shirt was worn by Alan Kelly for the Republic of Ireland. He made 47 appearances, the first against West Germany in 1957 and the last against Norway in 1973. Yellow shirts were once a common sight in international matches. Green was not an option for the Irish goalkeeper because the strip of the Irish team is green.

GOALIE'S GLOVES
Until the 1970s, gloves were worn only when it was wet, and they were made of thin cotton. Modern goalkeepers wear gloves in all conditions. Various coatings and pads are used to increase the gloves' grip, which is the key to handling the ball.

Goalkeepers may still wear a cap if the sun is in their eyes

Arms are outstretched, ready to block a shot

NARROWING THE ANGLE

This image from the 1930s shows a goalkeeper alert to danger. When an attacker approaches the goal with the ball, goalkeepers should leave their line and move towards the ball to reduce the target area for the attacker. This "narrowing of the angle" is an important part of keepers' roles. They often make marks, in line with the posts, to help them keep their bearings when leaving the line.

LOUD AND CLEAR

Italy's and Juventus's exceptional goalkeeper Gianluigi Buffon controls his penalty area by shouting instructions to his team-mates. This loud communication ensures the defenders line up in the best way to create a wall for a free kick or organize themselves effectively in the penalty area for a corner kick.

Goalkeepers shout at their team-mates to get the best protection during set pieces

Goalkeepers have to point when organizing the defensive wall for a free kick

THROWING OUT

This painted button from the 1900s shows one of the goalkeeper's jobs. A quick throw out, particularly after catching a corner, can be an effective way of launching an attack. Some goalkeepers are renowned for the length of their throw.

GOAL KICK

When the ball is put out behind the goal-line by an attacker, the opposing team is awarded a goal kick. The goalkeeper takes the kick from inside the 6-yard (5.5-m) box. Early leather balls absorbed water and increased in weight, so a goal kick rarely reached the opposition's half.

Tactics

Old Arabic print of team formations

P<small>ART OF FOOTBALL'S</small> appeal is its tactical element. Coaches and managers try to outwit the opposition by keeping their tactics secret until the match. Since football first began, teams have lined up in different formations trying to play in a way that will take the other team by surprise and result in a goal. Early players had the physical attributes and skills needed for a particular position on the field. Today, the pace of the game demands that players be adaptable enough to play in almost any position, in the manner of the Dutch "total football" teams of the 1970s.

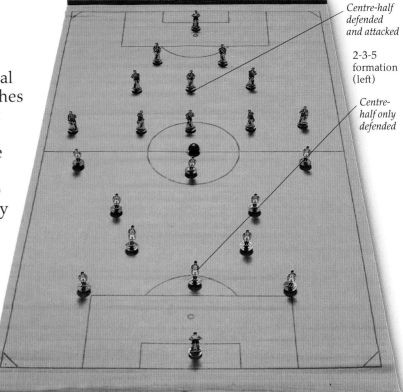

Centre-half defended and attacked

2-3-5 formation (left)

Centre-half only defended

W-M formation (right)

France won the 1998 World Cup with a back four

Wingers have been replaced by midfielders who can also defend

4-4-2 formation (right)

One forward often plays "in the hole" behind the other

Wing-backs are responsible for providing attacking width

Sweeper must be creative and pass accurately

Sweeper system (left)

IN GOOD FORM (ABOVE)
The 2-3-5 formation dominated tactics until the 1930s. Each player had a very specific place and role on the pitch. Herbert Chapman of Arsenal, England, was the first manager to make a radical change, positioning the centre-half and inside-forwards deeper to create the W-M formation.

GAME PLAN (ABOVE)
In recent years, software companies have developed computer programs that enable managers to plan their tactics on-screen. The 4-3-3 formation shown here is one of the most frequently used in modern football.

CLEAN SWEEP
Modern formations are very varied, but the 4-4-2 is one of the most popular. The four defenders are not expected to push forwards and the four midfielders sometimes switch to a diamond shape. The sweeper system, perfected by the Italians in the 1960s, frees one player from marking duties to act as cover.

PACKED DEFENCE

Denial of space to the opposition forwards is vital and certain players may be singled out for man-to-man marking. It is often said that the best teams are built from the back, with a strong defence providing a springboard for attack. Here, England defenders are surrounding a striker.

The defenders are physically blocking in the attacker

The attacker is trapped

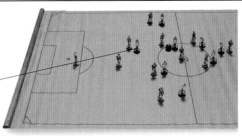

The forward cannot go "one on one" with the goalkeeper

OFFSIDE ORIGINS

The first offside law, in 1866, stated that three defenders, including the goalkeeper, had to be between the attacker and the goal when the ball was being played forwards by a team-mate. By 1920, fewer and fewer goals were being scored because, even if attackers were onside at the vital point, they still had to beat the last outfield defender.

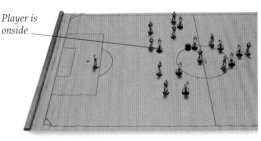

Player is onside

OFFSIDE UPDATED

In 1925, FIFA decided to amend the offside law so that only two players had to be between the attacker and the goal. Immediately, far more goals were scored. The offside rule is basically unchanged today. Here, the midfielder is about to pass the ball to the forward. This player is still onside and, once in possession of the ball, will have only the goalkeeper to beat.

Player is offside

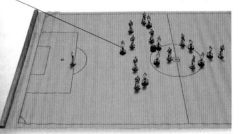

OFFSIDE TRAP

Teams without a sweeper, like Norway under Egil Olsen, are still able to use an offside trap. As the midfielder prepares to pass the ball forwards, the defenders suddenly advance up the field in a line, leaving the forward offside when the ball is played. William McCracken of Newcastle, England, was famous for first perfecting this tactic, in the years before World War I.

NO SUBSTITUTE

Substitutions were first allowed by FIFA in 1923, but only if a player was injured. Injuries were faked so often to let coaches make tactical changes that it was gradually accepted that one player could be freely replaced. Now the number of substitutes allowed per team has increased to seven for many games.

BE PREPARED

Javier Zanetti's goal for Argentina against England at France '98 was an example of how a well-rehearsed routine can work brilliantly. Lots of goals are scored from set-pieces – movements that a team practises before a match. Coaches spend a great deal of time going through these with the team in training.

Injury time

Mr Black the footballer from a Happy Families card game

A PROFESSIONAL FOOTBALLER'S job involves far more than playing matches and enjoying the limelight. Training, fitness, and recovery from injuries are day-to-day concerns for the modern player. Advances in medicine mean that injuries that a few years ago would have led to inevitable retirement can now be successfully treated. The pace of the modern game is unrelenting and loss of fitness is likely to stop a player from staying at the top level. Physiotherapy, nutrition, and even psychology are all parts of the conditioning programme of big clubs today.

FIGHTING FIT
Medicine balls like this were used in football training for many decades. They are extremely heavy, so throwing them improves stamina and also builds muscle bulk. Sophisticated gym equipment, training programmes, and resistance machines are now commonly used. Strength and fitness are essential to success in the modern game because top players have to play as many as 70 games per season. The greatest players are superb athletes as much as they are skilled footballers.

VITAL EDGE
Vittorio Pozzo, one of the first great managers, led Italy to victory in the World Cup in 1934 and 1938. He realized the importance of physical fitness and made his team train hard to give them a vital edge over their opponents. This paid off in extra time in the 1934 final, when Italy eventually scored the winning goal.

WARM UP AND COOL DOWN
A proper match-day routine can help to prolong a player's footballing career. Modern players are aware of the importance of warming up thoroughly before a game. The risk of muscle tears and strains is significantly reduced if the muscles are warm and loose. Recovery after games is also important. Many teams "warm down" after a match to relax their muscles before resting them.

The stretcher is carried by two wooden poles

A pillow is built into the stretcher

A piece of canvas supports the injured player

GETTING CARRIED AWAY
This stretcher was used in the 1920s. In those days, if the stretcher was brought out on the pitch, the crowd knew that a player was seriously injured. Today, players are given a few moments to get up before they are carried off to prevent time-wasting and a delay to the game. They often run on again shortly afterwards. In many countries, motorized buggies or carts have taken the place of traditional stretchers.

AS IF BY MAGIC
The "magic" sponge has a special place in football folklore. Spectators have often wondered how a rub down with a sponge and cold water could result in a player's swift recovery from an injury. Today, the team physiotherapist, rather than the trainer, treats players for injury problems on the pitch and off it. Physiotherapists are fully qualified to give sophisticated treatment to injured players.

The sponge is still used in amateur games

SOLDIERING ON

Injured players are usually substituted to prevent them doing more damage, but some injuries do not need to stop a player from turning out for an important match. Former England defender Terry Butcher, left, played with a badly cut head and bloodstained shirt during a vital World Cup qualifier in Sweden on 6 September 1989. Today, players must leave the pitch for treatment if they are bleeding from an injury sustained during a game.

The physiotherapist carries plenty of equipment onto the pitch

Physio's security pass

Modern medicine cases are light and waterproof

PITCH DOCTOR

Nigeria's Daniel Amokachi is shown here being treated for a hamstring injury during a 1994 World Cup match. The hamstring muscle, at the back of the leg, is one of the most vulnerable for a footballer. Straining it usually results in a three to four-week lay-off.

Ice is applied to the injury to reduce inflammation

The bag is made of leather

LOTIONS AND POTIONS

This medicine bag belonged to Ramsgate FC in the early 20th century. They were a non-League team from Kent in England. The bottles would have contained various lotions and medicines to warm muscles, pour on grazes, or reduce pain. Professional clubs in many countries are now required to have a doctor on hand at every game to deal with serious head injuries and fractures.

The trainer's medicines sometimes included chloroform to sedate a badly injured player

Footballs

An 1890s brass travelling inkwell in the shape of a football

MUCH OF THE APPEAL of football lies in the fact that it can be played without any special equipment. Children everywhere know that a tin can, some bound-up rags, or a ball from a different sport entirely, can be satisfyingly kicked around. This ingenuity was first displayed hundreds of years ago, when people discovered that an animal's bladder could be inflated and knotted to provide a light, bouncy ball. A bladder alone did not last very long when kicked, so people began to protect the bladders in a shell made of animal skin cured to turn it into leather. This design worked so well that it is still used today but with modern, synthetic materials rather than animal products.

HEAVY GOING
Balls of the 1870s were often formed by stitching together eight segments of leather, the ends of which were secured by a central disc. The leather was unprotected and could absorb water on wet days, so that the ball increased in weight. Heading the ball could be dangerous, even fatal, and so this technique was not often used in those days. The dribbling game was the popular style and the heavy ball was suitable for this style of play.

Manufacturers' names were first stencilled on balls in about 1900

Sections of leather sewn together

The lace for tightening the case stands proud

Interlocking panels of leather

Tool for lacing the ball tightly

Copper stencil

MADE TO MEASURE
This ball was used in March 1912, in the international match between Wales and England at Wrexham, Wales. England won the match 2–0. Made from a pig's bladder wrapped in cowhide, it is typical of the type of ball used for most of the 20th century. The outside shell was laced up. The size and weight of footballs were standardized for the first FA Challenge Cup competition in 1872 but the balls still absorbed water and were prone to losing their shape.

The colours are based on the French flag

Brand name marked on the ball with a stencil

WORLD CUP COLOURS
The first World Cup balls to have a colour other than black were used in the Finals in France in 1998. They had a shiny, synthetic coating to make them waterproof and incorporated a layer of foam between the latex bladder and polyester skin. This let players pass and shoot quickly and also put spin and swerve on the ball. Like 75 per cent of the world's footballs, they were made in the Sialkot region of Pakistan.

HEADING FOR TROUBLE
Balls like this were used in the 1966 World Cup Finals, at which time ball design had hardly changed in 50 years. The leather case was backed with a lining, a development of the 1940s that improved durability. The outside was painted with a pigment that helped to repel some water from a rain-soaked pitch. Manufacturers had still not found a reliable alternative to lacing up the ball so players risked injury when they headed the ball.

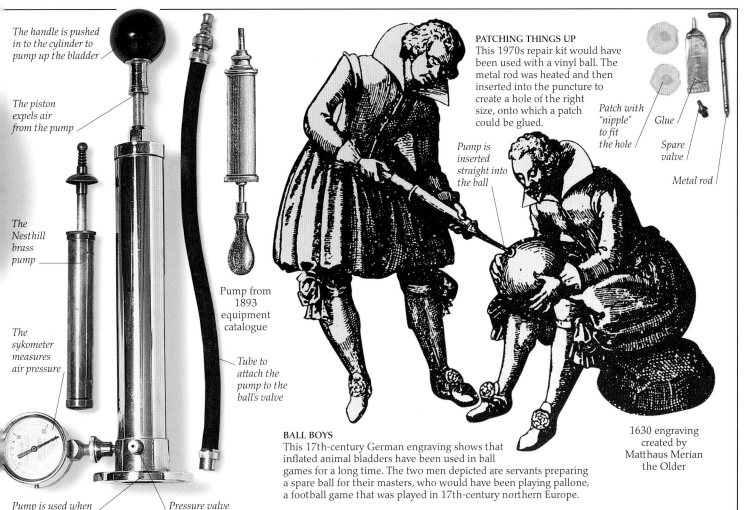

The handle is pushed in to the cylinder to pump up the bladder

The piston expels air from the pump

The Nesthill brass pump

The sykometer measures air pressure

Pump is used when standing upright

Pressure valve

Pump from 1893 equipment catalogue

Tube to attach the pump to the ball's valve

PATCHING THINGS UP
This 1970s repair kit would have been used with a vinyl ball. The metal rod was heated and then inserted into the puncture to create a hole of the right size, onto which a patch could be glued.

Pump is inserted straight into the ball

Patch with "nipple" to fit the hole

Glue

Spare valve

Metal rod

BALL BOYS
This 17th-century German engraving shows that inflated animal bladders have been used in ball games for a long time. The two men depicted are servants preparing a spare ball for their masters, who would have been playing pallone, a football game that was played in 17th-century northern Europe.

1630 engraving created by Matthaus Merian the Older

FULL OF AIR
Over time, air escaped from a football's bladder and a pump was used to reinflate it. Sometimes, the air pressure in a bladder was increased to improve the bounce of the ball. If a bladder was pumped up too high it was likely to burst, so some pumps came with their own pressure gauge. These pumps date from the 1890s.

Calcio balls are made of leather that is stitched together and then painted

The use of two colours makes the Orkney ball flash in the air

Alternative balls

Several different football games are played around the world today. They each use a ball particular to that game. Some football games have existed for centuries. The balls may have features connected to a ceremonial aspect of the game, and involve decoration and colour, or they may be designed to withstand harsh treatment. In some modern games the ball has evolved along with the game.

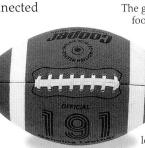

SHAPING UP
The game of American football was originally based on kicking a ball. As throwing became a central feature, the present shape of the ball evolved. The small ball can be gripped firmly, making it easier for the quarterback to make long, accurate passes.

BUILT TO LAST
In the Scottish Orkney Isles, a type of football game is played through the streets every New Year. The ball is much heavier than a normal football and is stuffed tightly with pieces of cork. This helps it to last for several hours of play and also makes it float on water – a useful feature because a team can score a goal by throwing the ball into the sea.

MADE TO MATCH
Calcio, first played in Italy in the 16th century, was reintroduced to Florence in 1930. The game is played by teams of 27 a side, all wearing medieval clothes and armour. Balls of various colours are used including green, white, and red to match the costumes. Calcio balls are smaller than regular footballs, making it easier for the players to pick them up and throw them.

Football boots

A 1950s painting of football boots called *Christopher's Boots*, by Doris Brand

O<small>F ALL FOOTBALL</small> equipment, boots have changed most over the last 100 years. Always the most expensive item of kit, they remain an unaffordable luxury to many players around the world who have to play in bare feet. The fast, agile sport we see today would simply not be possible if football players had to use the heavy, cumbersome boots worn up until the 1930s. Professionals then dreaded having to "break in" hard, new boots, which involved a great deal of pain. They preferred to patch up an old pair again and again until they fell apart. In the first World Cup tournaments in the 1930s, the South American teams wore lighter, low-cut boots, much to the astonishment of the Europeans. These began the trend towards the modern, high-tech boot.

MULTI-PURPOSE BOOTS
In the late 1800s, very few people playing football would have had specialist footwear. These girls' boots could also have been worn to school or in the house. The smooth soles, pronounced heel, and extremely high cut would have seriously constricted movement, but the ankle would have been well protected.

19th-century girls' boots

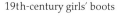

1920s child's boots

A "kick around" is a popular pastime with children

MADE FOR THE JOB
By the 1920s, football boots like the "Manfield Hotspur" were being mass-produced for footballers of all ages. Children's boots were designed just like adults', with reinforced toecaps and heels, some ankle protection, and leather studs. Social conditions at the time, though, meant that most working-class families could not afford such equipment and, if they could, they would have handed down boots from one child to another.

Extra foot support

Cotton laces

STUDLESS BOOTS
A 19th-century gentleman footballer wore studless boots, which would not have allowed for sharp turns or long passing. However, they were practical enough for the type of dribbling game favoured by the great English amateur teams like the Corinthians. This style of play was dictated by the confined spaces used for football practice at many British public schools. Boots like these would have doubled in weight when wet.

BOOTS IN THE BATH
In 1910 these boots were marketed as "Cup Final Specials", an early example of a football product being tied to a famous match. The wickerwork pattern on the toes was one of several designs that were thought to help a player control the ball – a major part of modern boot design too. It was common for a player to wear a new pair of boots in the bath for a few hours to soften the leather.

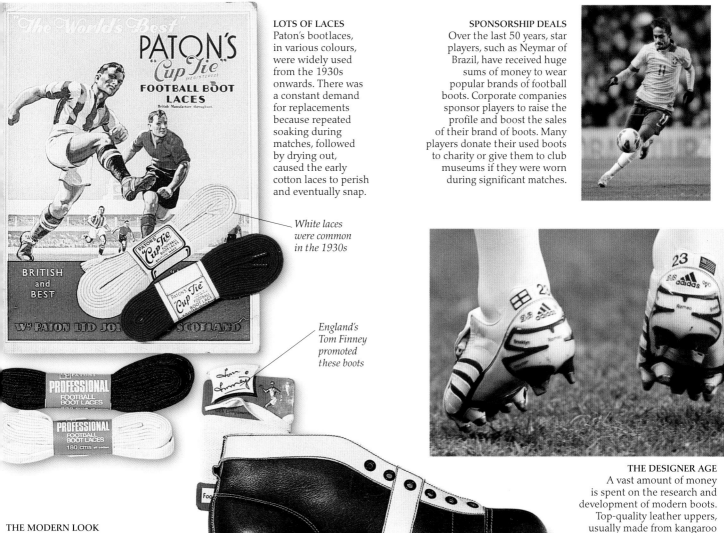

LOTS OF LACES
Paton's bootlaces, in various colours, were widely used from the 1930s onwards. There was a constant demand for replacements because repeated soaking during matches, followed by drying out, caused the early cotton laces to perish and eventually snap.

SPONSORSHIP DEALS
Over the last 50 years, star players, such as Neymar of Brazil, have received huge sums of money to wear popular brands of football boots. Corporate companies sponsor players to raise the profile and boost the sales of their brand of boots. Many players donate their used boots to charity or give them to club museums if they were worn during significant matches.

White laces were common in the 1930s

England's Tom Finney promoted these boots

THE DESIGNER AGE
A vast amount of money is spent on the research and development of modern boots. Top-quality leather uppers, usually made from kangaroo hides, and light, synthetic soles combine to make boots that last. They are comfortable and allow the best players to put amazing amounts of spin on the ball. Former England captain David Beckham wore a new pair of boots for every game. This pair was specially designed to include the names of his sons.

THE MODERN LOOK
The classic black-with-white-trim design, which is still used today, became popular in the 1950s. The vertical strap on the instep remains from earlier designs. The boots were becoming flexible enough to be worn without much breaking-in. There was less protection around the ankle, which allowed players more freedom of movement but led to an increase in injuries. It was at this time that bootmakers began to use the name of famous players to sell their boots.

Studs and stuff

The number of studs on the sole, and the way in which they are positioned, varies greatly. Longer studs are needed if the pitch is wet and muddy, shorter ones are worn if the pitch is hard. Modern boots often feature studs of a fixed length that are moulded to the sole of the boot. The potential of studs to cause injury has always been a concern to the game's governing bodies and one of the jobs of the referee or assistant is to check the studs of every player entering the field of play.

Studs are screwed into the sole

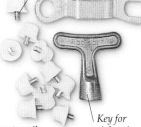

Wooden hammer

Nails fixed to studs

Separate nails

Key for tightening the studs

THE FIRST STUDS
Early football boots were made entirely of leather. The studs had to be hammered into the soles.

HARMFUL HAMMERS
Rubber studs came next. They also needed nailing to the sole and it was not long before the boots were damaged.

ALL CHANGE!
Modern screw-in studs are made of plastic or metal. Players can change their studs at half-time, to adjust to changes in conditions.

Football outfits

In the 19th century, both football and rugby players wore knee-length knickerbockers with no leg protection

Shirts, shorts, and socks were described as the basis of a footballer's outfit in the first Laws of 1863 and they remain so today. The materials used for a footballer's outfit have changed since then. Players in South America and Mediterranean countries needed clothing suitable for warm climates, so wool gave way to cotton and then artificial fibres. Cool fabrics that "breathe" are now the norm worldwide. Teams wear matching outfits, or strips, on the field of play. The colours are the club colours, with which all the fans can identify. Most clubs and international sides have a home and an away strip in case two teams wear the same colours.

DUTCH ORANGE
The Holland strip is unusual in being orange, and is recognized all around the world. The Dutch fans wear replica shirts and other orange clothes to form a mass of colour at matches. Here, striker Klaas-Jan Huntelaar, nicknamed The Hunter, wears his national side's distinctive kit.

WOOLLY JUMPERS
In the late 19th century, football jerseys were often made from wool. They tended to stretch out of shape and could become heavy in the rain because they soaked up water.

AWAY STRIP
In the 1966 World Cup final, the England team wore cotton shirts with a round collar. Although England were playing at home, they did not wear their normal white home strip because West Germany were wearing white. They wore red instead.

LACE-UPS
At all levels of the game, teams began to wear matching strips. This black-and-white shirt was worn by a member of Newcastle United's team for the 1908 English FA Cup final. Newcastle still wear black-and-white today. The shirt is made of thick cotton with a lace-up collar. Lace-up collars became fashionable again in the 1990s and were worn by Manchester United, among other teams.

AUSTRALIAN AMATEURS
This Australian shirt is made from wool with a cotton collar. It was worn in 1925 by the player Tommy Traynor. Shirts worn in international matches have symbolic importance. At the end of the game, the teams swap shirts with each other in a gesture of goodwill.

KEEPING COOL
Today, most shirts are designed to keep players cool and draw away excess moisture. This 1994 Brazil World Cup shirt is made of light, synthetic fabrics. With the energetic pace of modern games, such improvements are vital, especially for matches played in hot climates.

FAIR-WEATHER FRIENDS

By the early 20th century, manufacturers in many countries had begun to adapt the kit that British players had taken overseas with them in the 19th century. They produced lighter outfits more suited to warm climates. Short-sleeved shirts and deep V-neck collars became part of the typical Mediterranean look, as represented on this image from Valencia in Spain.

Early 1900s Spanish illustration

These socks are unusually decorative

Women were not expected to head the ball

Hoops and stripes are classic design features

PULL YOUR SOCKS UP

These socks from the 1920s look just the same as modern ones but they are made of wool. Modern socks are made of synthetic materials, making them more comfortable. Players keep their socks up with ties around the top. The ties can be made from strips of bandage or elasticated tape cut up into lengths. Towards the end of a gruelling match, when players are prone to cramp, they may discard the tie-ups. Socks around the ankle can be a tell-tale sign of a tired footballer facing defeat.

High kicking was easier if shorts were above the knees

Cream flannel shorts from about 1900

Modern synthetic shorts with decorative side seams

Hard-wearing cotton shorts from the 1930s

Early 20th-century French illustration

SHORT STORY

Amateurs in the 1860s played in full-length trousers but, as the game developed, players had to increase their speed and agility. Shorter knickerbockers cut just above the knee became popular. The baggy style of football shorts of the 1930s was made famous by Alex James of Arsenal, England, "the wee man in the big shorts". This fashion was revived in the 1990s following a trend in the 1970s and 1980s for tight shorts.

UNDER WRAPS

Until World War I, women footballers had to keep their hair under a cap or bonnet and hide their legs inside voluminous bloomers. In the 1910s, when many men were away at war, crowds flocked to see women's exhibition matches. This wider acceptance of ladies' football enabled women's teams to start wearing football outfits that were similar to those worn by men and more suitable for the game.

Accessories

Catalogue illustration of protective ear-muffs

INJURY AND DISCOMFORT were part of the game of football in its early days. When protective equipment and other accessories, such as hats, ear-muffs, and belts, were introduced at the end of the 19th century, they helped to distance the game from its rather violent past. Shin-pads were developed in 1874 by Nottingham Forest's Samuel Widdowson in response to the physical punishment that players suffered during games. Leg protection is still part of kit today, but other accessories are no longer used.

Buttoned tunic was an alternative to the more common shirt

Leather buckles fasten these shin-pads

LASTING DESIGN
In the 1900s, players would have worn shin-pads like these outside their socks, held in place with straps and buckles. The front section is made of leather and the back of cotton, with a stuffing in between of animal hair. This mix of materials was used in shin-pads until the 1960s.

THE FIRST SHIN-PADS
The earliest shin-pads were worn outside the socks and were extended to include ankle protectors, which rested on the top of the boot. Some, like these, had a suede covering, which was more prone to water damage than other types of leather. These heavy and inflexible pads date from the 1890s, about 20 years after shin-pads became part of the footballer's kit.

REINFORCED GUARDS
This figure is from a picture on the box of a late 19th-century German football game. His shin-pads, worn over the top of his socks and knickerbockers, appear to be strengthened with cane bars.

BELT UP
Decorative belts were a part of many schoolboys' football kits until the 20th century. They smartened up appearances by holding in the shirt and gave teams identity through the use of colours. Belts were also part of women's kit in the early 1900s.

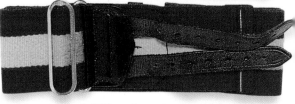

Early 20th-century schoolboys' belts

Woman's belt from 1895

1980s shin-pads were similar in shape to those from the 1930s

Long laces to wrap twice around the leg

ROOM TO MOVE
By 1910, ankle protection was no longer part of shin-pad design, not because it was not needed, but because it restricted movement of the foot. Passing and running off the ball had become important parts of the game, requiring increased flexibility of the ankle. Players were therefore forced to sacrifice some protection. Cork was sometimes used to strengthen pads.

TIE-ON SHIN-PADS
Shin-pads worn inside the socks had taken over by 1930. Laces were used for fastening instead of buckles, to prevent chafing on the players' legs. Many years later, tighter-fitting synthetic, rather than woollen, socks held the pads firmly in position without the need for ties of any sort.

LIGHTWEIGHT PROTECTION
Modern shin-pads look dramatically different from earlier models. They are shaped to fit the leg, using lightweight materials to give excellent protection. Even the delicate Achilles tendon at the back of the ankle is shielded. The revival of ankle protectors, after a gap of 100 years, brings shin-pad design full circle.

Ladies wore hats to keep long hair out of the mud

KEEPING WARM
Gloves have become common, especially among players from hot countries who play in Europe, often in freezing temperatures. Players susceptible to hamstring and groin injuries are encouraged to wear undershorts because they help to keep these important muscles warm.

Stripes to match team colours

Women's football hats

FOOTBALL FIGURE
This porcelain figure of a boy was made in Germany in the 1890s. Artistic depictions of football from this period often showed players wearing hats, even though they were becoming decorative rather than practical items.

Hand-painted German figure

Brazilian footballer Gilberto Silva

HATS OFF!
These women's hats date from 1895, when ladies' football was still in its infancy. The fact that women played in hats does not mean that theirs was a gentler game. Like the men, many female players wore shin-pads for protection.

Famous players

Fᴏᴏᴛʙᴀʟʟ ɪꜱ ᴀ ᴛᴇᴀᴍ ɢᴀᴍᴇ. Clubs and national sides inspire the greatest passion among fans but a few players are so gifted and entertaining that they stand out from their team-mates and draw thousands of extra people to matches. Some great players are famous for their spirit of fair play while others have been surrounded by controversy and bad publicity. But all of the great players share an ability to change the course of a match through a moment of incredible individual skill.

GORDON BANKS (b. 1937)
English goalkeeper Gordon Banks is remembered for one save in particular – a spectacular effort that kept out Pelé's header in the 1970 World Cup. Banks won 73 caps between 1963 and 1972 and would have won more, but for an eye injury.

JOHANN CRUYFF (b. 1947)
One of the few great players also to have become a successful manager, Cruyff was able to instil in his teams some of the style and tactical awareness that made him such a joy to watch. He played for Holland, Ajax, and Barcelona, Spain. He personified the concept of "total football" by floating all over the pitch and using his amazing balance and skill to open up defences.

GERD MULLER (b. 1945)
Known as *"Der Bomber"*, Gerd Muller was an unlikely looking centre-forward. He had an astonishing spring in his heels, which made up for his lack of height. He was a prolific goal scorer, with 68 goals in 62 games for West Germany. Most of his club football was played with Bayern Munich, Germany, for whom he scored a record 365 goals.

Milla was a great entertainer, known for his flamboyant goal celebrations

Roger Milla after scoring for Cameroon against Colombia in the 1990 World Cup

ROGER MILLA (b. 1952)
Twice African Player of the Year, Roger Milla of Cameroon was the first player to become famous worldwide playing for an African country. He was also the oldest player to appear and score in a World Cup match in 1994, aged 42.

BOBBY CHARLTON (b. 1937)
Manchester United star Bobby Charlton survived the Munich air crash that killed eight of his team-mates in 1958. Known for the power and accuracy of his shooting, he was invaluable in England's 1966 World Cup win. He was knighted in 1994.

Eusébio practises ball control in training

Eusébio scored 38 goals in 46 internationals

DIEGO MARADONA (b. 1960)
Maradona was the best player of his generation and also one of the most controversial. He had a tremendous ability to inspire his team-mates, most notably when leading Argentina to the 1986 World Cup and Napoli to two Series A titles in Italy in the late 1980s. His magical left foot and strength in possession were his main assets.

Maradona's low centre of gravity gave him excellent balance

In the 1986 World Cup against England, Maradona scored two goals – one a handball that should have been disallowed, the other a dazzling solo effort

EUSÉBIO (b. 1942)
Although he was born in Mozambique, Eusébio was snapped up by Benfica of Lisbon, Portugal, and went on to play for Portugal, in common with several other talented players. He starred in the 1962 European Cup final, scoring twice as Benfica beat Real Madrid, Spain, 5–3. Eusébio was respected all over the world for his fair play and dignity as well as for his footballing talent.

Meazza (below right) shakes hands with Hungarian captain, Sarosi, before the 1938 World Cup Final

Like many of the greatest players, Maradona liked to be number 10

GARRINCHA (1933–83)
Nicknamed "the Little Bird", Garrincha had polio as a child. He overcame his disability to become one of the quickest and most elusive wingers the game has seen. He played on the right-hand side of Brazil's legendary 1958 forward line. In 1962, he made up for the absence of the injured Pelé with some brilliant performances, helping Brazil to retain the World Cup.

Maradona's magical footwork entertained and amazed the fans

GIUSEPPE MEAZZA (1910–79)
Italian Giuseppe Meazza won two World Cup winner's medals in 1934 and 1938. He was respected as a creator and scorer of goals from his inside-forward position. In 1938, he organized the Italian team when the coach, Pozzo, was ordered to leave the bench and sit in the stands. He spent his best years at Internazionale of Milan, Italy, and won 53 caps.

Continued on next page

LIONEL MESSI (b. 1987)
A skillful forward, Lionel Messi made his competitive debut for Barcelona at the age of 16 and has since won six Spanish league championships with the club. The captain of Argentina, he won the FIFA Ballon d'Or – awarded to the best player in the world – three times in a row between 2010 and 2012.

LUIS SUÁREZ (b. 1935)
Considered one of the best-ever Spanish footballers, Luis Suárez dominated the midfield for Barcelona, Spain, in the late 1950s. By the mid-1960s, he was playing a key part in Italian Inter Milan's new *catenaccio* system – a line-up heavy on defence with only two forward players. He was famous for his fast breaks out of defence and accurate passes. Suárez went on to be manager of Spain at the 1990 World Cup.

Zidane combined balance with strength to provide a complete attacking threat

Messi's delicate touch and close control make him one of the world's best dribblers

ZINEDINE ZIDANE (b. 1972)
One of the greatest players of modern times, the French attacking midfielder Zinedine Zidane combined physical strength with skill and intelligence. In 1998, he propelled France to their first World Cup win with two goals against Brazil in the final. He also helped Real Madrid to victory in the 2002 Champions League final with a man-of-the-match performance.

The two defenders are playing for the Italian club Roma

Roma defenders are left in Platini's wake

STANLEY MATTHEWS (1915–2000)
England's Stanley Matthews was known for his dribbling skills. One of his finest performances was in Blackpool's 4–3 win over Bolton in the 1953 English FA Cup final. He won 84 caps and played his last game for Stoke City at the age of 50. He was knighted in 1965.

LEV YASHIN (1929–90)
Always kitted out in black, Lev Yashin was rivalled only by Gordon Banks as the greatest goalkeeper of his era. He played for the Soviet Union in three World Cups and is, to this day, the only goalkeeper to have been named European Footballer of the Year.

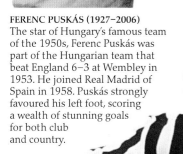

Between them, Puskás and Di Stéfano scored seven goals in the European Cup final in 1960

FRANZ BECKENBAUER (b. 1945)

Beckenbauer's intelligence shone out on the field as he dictated play from a deep sweeper position. Together with Johann Cruyff, he is one of the few football-playing legends to achieve similar success as a manager. Having captained West Germany at the 1974 World Cup, he managed them when they won again in 1990.

FERENC PUSKÁS (1927–2006)

The star of Hungary's famous team of the 1950s, Ferenc Puskás was part of the Hungarian team that beat England 6–3 at Wembley in 1953. He joined Real Madrid of Spain in 1958. Puskás strongly favoured his left foot, scoring a wealth of stunning goals for both club and country.

ALFREDO DI STÉFANO (b. 1926)

When Real Madrid dominated European football in the 1950s, Di Stéfano was one of their star players. His stamina enabled him to contribute all over the field. He and Puskás formed one of football's legendary double acts.

MICHEL PLATINI (b. 1955)

Platini was one of those players who seemed happy to take the weight of a nation's expectations on his shoulders. He captained France in the 1984 European Championships, and they won the tournament for the first time. Platini was an attacking midfielder who often finished as top scorer at Italian club Juventus.

Michel Platini playing for Juventus

Platini had the speed and foresight to move forwards into space

PELÉ (b. 1940)

Many people's choice of the greatest player of all, Pelé was king of Brazilian football from the late 1950s to the early 1970s. He overcame constant fouling by frustrated defenders to score more than 1,000 goals for Brazilian club Santos, American soccer team New York Cosmos, and the Brazilian national team. His enthusiasm and obvious love of playing, despite being plagued by injury, make him a perfect role model for the game of football.

Medals and caps

Sew-on badge given to members of an international squad

IT IS THE AIM OF ALL footballers to play well and win each game. Those lucky enough to win a championship are awarded a medal as a mark of their achievement. Those good enough to be picked to play for their country win a cap. Medals and caps have been part of the game since the 19th century and are still highly valued rewards today. At the highest level, success can be measured by the number of caps a player has and passing the "100 cap" mark is considered exceptional service to the national team. Vitālijs Astafjevs of Latvia won 167 caps – a record for a European.

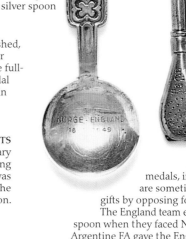

Argentine pot made from a dried aubergine trimmed with silver

Ornate silver dagger

Norwegian silver spoon

Argentine silver spoon

Medals

As with military medals for soldiers, footballers are rewarded with medals for helping their side, not for a moment of personal glory. Medals are awarded at all levels of football, professional and amateur. They are mementos by which players can remember their glory days and can become valuable collectors' items.

GOOD SPORT
Before organized leagues were established, football medals were often awarded for sportsmanship as well as victories. The full-back C Duckworth was given this medal for "gentlemanly and successful play" in the 1883–84 season.

WITH COMPLIMENTS
This "complimentary medal for defeating all comers" was awarded in the 1884–85 season.

PRECIOUS GIFTS
As well as caps and medals, international players are sometimes presented with gifts by opposing football associations. The England team each received a silver spoon when they faced Norway in 1949. The Argentine FA gave the English team members ceremonial daggers and other silver items on their first visit to Wembley, England, in 1951.

CLUB STRIKERS
Some clubs strike their own medals to mark a special achievement of their players. This medal was awarded at the end of a season to players of a team that had won its league.

Lancashire Cup winners 1887

English v Scottish League 1893

FA Cup runners-up 1893

DOUBLE
This group of medals belonged to R H Howarth of the Preston North End "Invincibles". The team won the League and the FA Cup in 1888–89, achieving the first English "double".

TROPHY TRIUMPH
This plaque was made to commemorate an international match between France and England in 1947. All the English players received a plaque after winning the match 3–0.

HUNGARY HIT
Hungary was one of the first European countries to take to football. They copied the way other countries organized the game, including the awarding of medals. This medal was awarded to the members of an international side after a match against Austria in 1909.

1909 Hungarian medal

CHAMPIONS
This medal was awarded to a player for success in the 1914–15 season.

AMATEUR
This 1920s medal was given to a successful amateur player.

ARSENAL STAR
This 1930s medal may have belonged to football star Alex James.

PLAY-OFF PRIZES
Medals have been presented to the winners of the third and fourth place play-off match at every World Cup Final, except 1930 and 1950. In the World Cup Final in Germany 2006, the host nation won third place medals, defeating Portugal 3–1.

Caps

A coloured cap was once the only way of showing to which side a player belonged. In 1872, the FA ruled that teams should wear distinctive shirts. In 1886, it was suggested that caps be awarded to footballers each time they played for their country. Today, they are given to every member of a national team, including playing substitutes. Often, only one cap is awarded for a series of games so a player with 50 "caps" may have fewer actual ones.

HOME CAP
This Welsh cap was awarded for the 1903–04 Home International matches between England, Scotland, Northern Ireland, and Wales. This tournament took place every year until 1984.

CAREY'S CAP
The great defender Johnny Carey won this cap when he played for Ireland against Poland and Switzerland in 1938. Carey won 36 caps.

Tassels are added for decoration

Welsh national crest – a dragon

1903-4

Details of matches can be embroidered into each panel

The date covers games from a whole season

Northern Ireland had its own team from 1921

Football caps are usually made from velvet

SCHOOL COLOURS
Football caps were first awarded in English public schools. "Colours", in the form of caps, were given to the most able players in each year.

IN TRAINING
It is not only players that are rewarded for their efforts. Trainer Will Scott received this medal when the English and Scottish Leagues met at Celtic Park, Glasgow, Scotland, in November 1931.

WAR GAMES
Throughout World War II, famous international players took part in exhibition matches arranged to boost public morale. In 1946, Tom Finney was given this set of three medals after appearing in a match in Antwerp, Belgium.

PROMOTIONAL MEDAL
By the 1950s, businesses had started to commemorate a range of football events. The French newspaper, *Le Soir*, made this medal to mark a club tour of Austria in 1953.

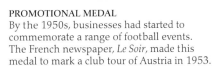

WORLD CUP
The biggest achievement in football is to win the World Cup. This is a spare Jules Rimet medal from the 1954 final, when West Germany beat the favourites, Hungary.

AFRICA CUP OF NATIONS
This medal was presented to the winners of the first Africa Cup of Nations. The competition was held in Khartoum, Sudan, and only Sudan, Ethiopia, and Egypt took part. Egypt beat Ethiopia 4–0 in the final.

Famous clubs

ITALIAN ZEBRAS
Juventus are the most successful Italian club and enjoy great support outside Turin. Nicknamed the Zebras for their black-and-white striped kit, they won the European Cup in 1985 and 1996.

CLUBS INSPIRE the greatest loyalty and passion from football fans, more so even than national teams. In every country, certain big clubs attract followers from beyond their local areas and tend to dominate their domestic leagues and cups. Success for these clubs often continues because financial backing ensures a steady supply of good new players. In all corners of the world, people swear allegiance to Barcelona or Liverpool, Flamengo or Milan, although they may never be able to attend a game involving their team.

BRAVO BENFICA
Only Porto and Sporting Lisbon rival Benfica in the Portuguese League. Benfica have also had some notable victories on the more competitive European stage. Benfica were the great team of the early 1960s, winning two European Cups, in 1961 and 1962, and reaching but losing three further finals.

This bronze depicts Benfica's symbol, an eagle

Figure of the ancient Greek hero Ajax forms the basis of the Dutch club's crest

BRILLIANT BARCELONA
In 2011, Barcelona, inspired by the precise and imaginative passing of the Spanish internationals Xavi and Andrés Iniesta, beat Manchester United 3–1 in the Champions League final. It was their second Champions League victory in three seasons and cemented their reputation as one of the greatest club sides in the history of European football.

LONDON LADIES
Netty Honeyball was the force behind the first great women's team in the 1890s. The British Ladies Club drew large crowds for their exhibition matches in London at a time when the capital was lagging behind the North and Midlands of England with regard to football.

YOUNG TALENT
In the 1970s, Dutch club Ajax's policy to develop their own young players bore fruit. The players, including the star Johann Cruyff, helped Ajax to three consecutive European Cup wins in the 1970s and some of them helped the national team in two World Cups. Despite regularly selling their best players, the club returned to the forefront of European football in the mid-1990s.

The club Ajax was formed in Amsterdam in 1900

BUSBY BABES
English club Manchester United started life as Newton Heath. They changed their name in 1902. The Munich air disaster of 1958, in which eight members of manager Matt Busby's young team died, inspired sympathy around the world. Since then, the club have won three European Cups – in 1968, 1999, and 2008.

Baines card from the 1890s shows full-back Jack Powell

PLAY UP NEWTON HEATH

POWELL

THE GOLDEN YEARS
Bayern Munich followed Ajax as the leading European team in the early 1970s. They won three consecutive European Cups with the help of players such as Franz Beckenbauer, Gerd Muller, and Sepp Maier, who were also important to the German national team.

Paul Breitner of Bayern Munich in 1974

Dominguez, the goalkeeper – from Argentina

Alfredo di Stéfano, the leader of the team

Francisco Gento, the fast left winger

REAL RIVALRY
In the late 1950s, Real Madrid, Spain, possibly had the greatest club side ever. Legends such as Di Stéfano and Puskás inspired this Spanish team to win the first five European Cups. Real Madrid have a spectacular stadium – the Bernabeu – and a bitter rivalry with Barcelona.

THE RED DEVILS
This picture shows the players Cagna and Rios of Independiente, Argentina, in 1995. In 1964, Independiente was the first Argentine club to win the South American club competition, the Copa Libertadores. The "Red Devils" went on to win the competition four more times between 1972 and 1975.

The fans

F OR ALL THE talent displayed by the players on the pitch, it is the fans who have made football the biggest game in the world. From the last years of the 19th century, working people began to have enough free time to attend sporting fixtures. They created an atmosphere of excitement and expectation, and large crowds became an important part of a match. Today, football is the most widely watched sport in the world. Fans are keener than ever to show their support for club and country in a range of noisy and colourful ways.

GONE BANANAS
In England in the late 1980s, there was a craze for taking large inflatables to matches. Fans waved bananas, fish, and fried eggs in the crowd to show their support for their teams.

Manchester City, England, pennant

Preston North End, England, rosette

Holland scarf

Lazio, Italy, scarf

PERFECT VIEW
In their desperation to see a game, fans are not always put off by the "ground full" signs. In the 19th century, before large-scale stands were built, trees provided a convenient spot from which to watch a popular match.

CLUB COLOURS
Colours are a vital part of the bond between a team and its supporters. Once, people made rosettes for big matches and displayed pennants. Now, fans often wear a scarf to show their loyalty.

RARE COLLECTION
Fans have always collected objects bearing images of football. Today, the items probably feature their favourite club but, in the past, designs were based on more general football scenes. Collecting autographs is also a popular hobby and offers a rare opportunity to meet star players.

John "Jack" Rowley, forward

John Aston, full-back

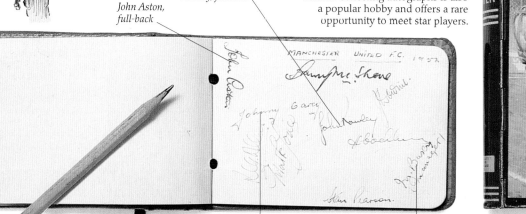

Johnny Carey, full-back

Matt Busby, manager

Child's money-box

1950s autograph book containing signatures of famous figures of Manchester United, England

Wooden pencil case

During the war, the sound of the bell warned people of an air-raid

Air-raid patrolman's rattle

Air-raid patrolman's bell

Rattles were originally used as bird scarers

Top section moves around and around horizontally

"Rattling" noise created at the handle

Adult's rattle

Child's rattle

NOISY SUPPORT

Rattles were part of the atmosphere at games until the 1960s. When the horizontal section of the rattle is whirled around the "clicker" on the handle, it produces a loud rattling noise. Since the 1960s, organized chanting has become more common. Modern safety regulations restrict what items may be taken into the stadium, and rattles are no longer allowed.

Child's rattle painted with a football scene

WAR CRY

Fans have taken bells and rattles to matches to express their support since before 1940. This bell and rattle were part of an air-raid patrolman's equipment in England during World War II. In 1946, after the war, a Derby County fan took them to matches during Derby's run to the English FA Cup final.

WORLD BEATERS

Brazilian fans were famous for their noisy support long before the rest of the world discovered paints and drums. They produce a samba beat on their drums and blow their whistles. As the noise echoes around the stands, the fans dance to accompany the action, especially if their team is winning.

AFRICAN PAINTING

Face-painting has become commonplace at major international matches, adding to the colour and spectacle of the occasion. Here, two Zambian fans, painted to reflect the team's colours, enjoy an Africa Cup of Nations match. Face-painting is particularly popular with Dutch, Danish, and Japanese fans.

Match day

This is a scoreboard from an early 20th-century French football game

THE ATMOSPHERE of a big game, the sound of the crowd, and the closeness of the players combine to make going to a live football match quite addictive. Even though football is now widely shown on television, millions of fans still go to the match. Many supporters, like players, are extremely superstitious and follow the same routine every time they go to a match. The crowd and the noisy support they give their team are essential to the game of football. It is vital that clubs continue to improve comfort and safety for their fans, so that they keep on coming back.

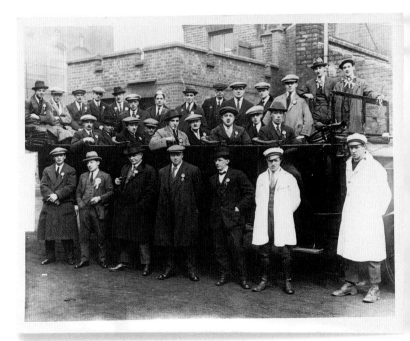

ALL DRESSED UP
This photo shows fans of West Ham, England, preparing to travel to the 1923 FA Cup final, the first to be held at Wembley. Many more than the official attendance of 123,000 crammed into the stadium. Notice the smart appearance of the supporters.

In the 1988 European Championship final, Holland beat the Soviet Union 2–0

Holograms and complicated designs are now used to deter ticket forgeries

TICKETS PLEASE
Tickets are essential in controlling access to games and keeping attendance to a safe level. Years ago, this was only necessary at cup finals and World Cup matches. Tickets were issued for general areas in the stadium. Now that terraces have been phased out in favour of seating, each match ticket corresponds to a particular seat.

READING MATTER
The earliest programmes were simple one-sheet items, giving only team line-ups. As football became more popular, further elements were added, such as a message from the manager and background information on the opposition. Glossy, full-colour brochures, largely paid for by advertising, are produced for tournaments such as the European Championships.

LET ME ENTERTAIN YOU
To make going to a match even more enjoyable, particularly for a family audience, clubs and governing bodies lay on extra entertainment before kick-off and at half-time. In the past, this may have taken the form of a brass band, but modern crowds expect something more elaborate. The opening ceremony at the World Cup Finals in Germany in 2006 featured Bavarian drummers and dancers lowered from the roof to the pitch.

MAJOR LEAGUE FUN
In the USA, a trip to a sporting event is usually a family day out, and the stadiums have good facilities for everybody. There is a lot of razzmatazz at the Major League Soccer matches. Cheerleaders and music keep the crowds well entertained. This is match day at the Vancouver Whitecaps' stadium.

1903 FA official's badge

Official badge from 1905

The badges are made of cloth and decorated with gold brocade

FA badge from 1898

The English three lions motif

Badge worn at 1899 England v Scotland international

ACCESS ALL AREAS?
Away from the mass of spectators, there are certain areas of the stadium, such as the boardroom, where access is strictly controlled. These badges, from 1898–1905, would have been sewn on blazers and worn by Football Association officials. These days, executive boxes have become a feature of many grounds.

CROWD CONTROL
Police and stewards attend football matches to ensure the safety of everybody at the game. Police, like these Italian officers at a Juventus match, may need to take a hard line with unruly fans, and sometimes use horses or dogs to help them control large crowds. They may also control traffic and escort supporters to and from the match.

COMING HOME
This drawing comes from a postcard from the early 20th century. The caption on the card says, "Our team's lost by ….. goals to …..". Space is left on the card for fans to fill in the score. Somehow, the depression of defeat is always replaced by excitement and high hopes when the next game comes around.

The stadium

WEMBLEY TOWERS
The famous towers at Wembley Stadium in England are sadly not part of the new 21st-century stadium.

AS CROWDS GREW EVER larger in the late 19th century, football clubs realized that they would have to build somewhere permanent to hold their matches. Stadiums became a necessity. They provided fans with shelter and a decent view of the game. They also created an atmosphere that added greatly to the matchday experience. A series of stadium disasters over the years, in places such as Scotland, Peru, and Russia, finally led to widespread belief that the terraces should be replaced by all-seater stands for the safety of spectators.

SHEFFIELD WEDNESDAY F.C.

THEN THERE WAS LIGHT...
Floodlights were first used in 1878 but they did not become standard at professional clubs until the 1950s. The most common form of stadium lighting was on tall pylons in the corners of the stadium. Today, lights are often placed in rows along the stand roof.

CROWD SAFETY
On 15 April 1989, the FA Cup semi-final at Hillsborough, Sheffield, was the scene of the worst disaster in English football history. Ninety-six Liverpool fans died as a result of a crowd crush. The report into the tragedy began a major leap forward in stadium safety, to prevent a similar disaster from ever happening again.

STATE OF THE ART
The new Wembley Stadium in north London took much longer than anticipated to erect and construction costs were considerably higher than initial estimates. Once it opened, however, the public flocked to this stunning stadium with its 90,000 capacity and giant screens, each the size of 600 television sets. The stadium boasts a fantastic steel arch that is lit up at night and can be seen right across the city.

Lights along the top of the roof

STANDING TALLER
Barcelona, Spain, moved from Les Corts Stadium to the spectacular Nou Camp in 1957. Improvements for the 1982 World Cup and 1992 Olympics have increased the staggering height of the stands. The Nou Camp was paid for by the club's members.

PATH TO THE PITCH
The tunnel is more than just a route on to the pitch. It is the place where players psych themselves up for the game and give in to their superstitions. Many insist on taking the same place in the line every time. Others put on their shirts only at the last moment.

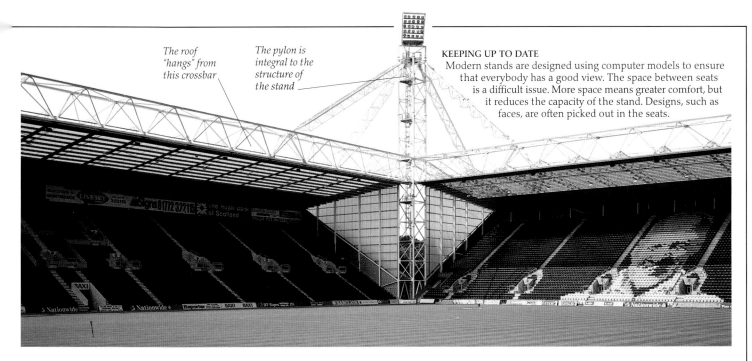

The roof "hangs" from this crossbar

The pylon is integral to the structure of the stand

KEEPING UP TO DATE
Modern stands are designed using computer models to ensure that everybody has a good view. The space between seats is a difficult issue. More space means greater comfort, but it reduces the capacity of the stand. Designs, such as faces, are often picked out in the seats.

FANS ON THEIR FEET
Before all-seater stadiums were introduced, fans stood packed together on terraces. Far more fans could get in to watch a match and it is how the majority of people have watched games for much of football's history. Children were often passed over the heads of the crowd to the front to give them a better view.

WORLD CUP WONDER
The Stade de France is in St Denis, north of Paris. It was built for the 1998 World Cup and 80,000 spectators watched the opening game there between Brazil and Scotland. The stadium was widely praised for its dramatic design. The roof, enclosing the ground in a continuous curve, creates an amphitheatre effect, which has always been popular in European and South American stadiums.

Several tiers of seats

Pitch-level openings for emergency vehicles

Revolving advertising hoardings around the pitch

The World Cup

THE FOOTBALL WORLD CUP is one of the greatest sporting events of our time. The first World Cup was held in Uruguay in 1930, 26 years after FIFA first discussed the idea. In the early days, some teams were unable to travel to the host country but, by the 1950s, long-distance travel was becoming much easier and quicker. As the tournament became more accessible, it grew in popularity. The 1950 World Cup Final at the Maracanã Stadium in Rio de Janeiro was attended by 200,000 people.

In 1958, Brazilian teenager Pelé became the first global football superstar. Since then, interest in the World Cup has boomed.

MANY MASCOTS
Every World Cup since 1966 has had a mascot. They appear as a life-size figure at matches and scaled-down promotional or commercial images. This is Pique, from Mexico '86.

WORLD FIRST
Uruguay offered to pay travel and accommodation expenses to the 13 visiting teams at the first World Cup. Only four European teams made the long journey, joining the seven South American teams.

1954 – Switzerland. West Germany beat Hungary 3–2 in one of the great upsets in World Cup history.

1958 – Sweden. Brazil beat Sweden 5–2. Brazil are the only team to have played in every Finals tournament.

1950 – Brazil. Uruguay beat Brazil 2–1, in the first tournament after World War II.

1962 – Chile. Brazil beat Czechoslovakia 3–1, with Garrincha taking centre stage after Pelé was injured.

1938 – France. Italy beat Hungary 4–2, inspired by their star inside-forward, Meazza.

1966 – England. West Germany lost 2–4 to England in extra time, with Geoff Hurst scoring the first hat-trick in a final.

1934 – Italy. Czechoslovakia lost 1–2 to Italy. Uruguay did not defend their crown, the only time this has happened.

1970 – Mexico. Brazil beat Italy 4–1 and were one of the greatest teams of all time.

1930 – Uruguay. Beating Argentina 4–2, Uruguay was the first of many host countries to win the Cup.

1974 – West Germany. Holland were beaten 2–1 by West Germany, who came back from being a goal behind.

VARIOUS VENUES
Many countries want to host this event as it attracts many visitors. The 2002 Finals, in Japan and South Korea, were the first shared tournament. In 2006, the Finals were held in Germany, and the 2010 Finals were staged in South Africa. Brazil are the hosts in 2014.

Argentina '78 is remembered for the ticker-tape in the River Plate Stadium

Mexico was the first country to host two Finals

The Italia '90 mascot was called Ciao

1978 – Argentina. Holland lost 1–3 to Argentina, leaving the Dutch as the best team never to have won the World Cup.

1982 – Spain. Italy beat West Germany 3–1, their striker Paolo Rossi finishing as leading scorer.

1986 – Mexico. Argentina beat West Germany 3–2, in a tournament dominated by Diego Maradona.

1990 – Italy. West Germany beat Argentina 1–0 in a defensive, bad-tempered final.

1998 – France. Brazil were beaten 3–0 by France in an amazingly one-sided match.

1994 – USA. Brazil beat Italy 3–2 on penalties after a 0–0 draw and became the only team to have won four World Cups.

The figure is a winged seraph

WANDERING TROPHY
The first World Cup trophy was designed by a French sculptor, Abel Lafleur. Originally named "Victory", it was later named in honour of the president of FIFA, Jules Rimet. The trophy was stolen before the 1966 tournament in England and was found in a park by a dog called Pickles. Brazil were presented with the trophy to keep in 1970 but, in 1983, it was stolen again and has not been seen since.

The trophy is made of solid gold

The engraving on the trophy is in French

COUPE DU MONDE
DE
FOOTBALL
ASSOCIATION
—
COUPE
JULES RIMET

Jules Rimet trophy

In 1994, American fans turned out in force to watch the matches

The fans at Italia '90 provided more drama than some of the matches

Sweden, the host team, made it to the final in 1958 but were overpowered by the Brazilian super-team

Copa del Mundo de la FIFA **Programma**

JULES RIMET CUP
WORLD CHAMPIONSHIP
ENGLAND 1966 JULY 11-30

ESPAÑA '82
EDICIÓN EXCLUSIVA PARA ESPAÑA

ITALIA 94

Guide
The World Championship in Football 1958
Sweden 8-29 · 6

STOCKHOLM
GOTEBORG
HALSINGBORG
MALMO

Coupe Jules Rimet

READ ALL ABOUT IT
Programmes for the World Cup are different from the club variety, in that they usually cover the whole tournament rather than a specific match. They contain information about the competing teams and are printed in several languages. These programmes are from Sweden '58, England '66, Spain '82, Italy '90, and USA '94.

Didi

Pelé was 17 in 1958

Garrincha

Vava played at centre-forward

Zagalo, the left-winger, scored the fourth goal in the final

THE BEAUTIFUL GAME
The 1958 final saw Brazil emerge as one of the World Cup's greatest-ever teams. Their forward line-up was among the strongest in the game's history. Garrincha, Didi, Vava, Pelé, and Zagalo drove the team to victory. Mario Zagalo later became the national team manager and was in charge when Brazil won again in 1970 and 1994.

Continued on next page

WE MUST HAVE THE WORLD CUP
This was the poster for the 1962 Finals in Chile. A series of earthquakes marred the run-up to the tournament but the hosts were determined. President of the Chilean FA, Carlos Dittborn, said "We have nothing. That is why we must have the World Cup." Chile overcame the doubts of some European teams by staging a successful event. There was more trouble on the pitch than off it, particularly in the "Battle of Santiago" between Italy and Chile. Italy finished the game with nine men.

Globe forms the top of the trophy

World Cup Willie inspired a World Cup theme song by Lonnie Donegan

The Union Jack flag represents Great Britain, not just England

Designed by Italian Silvio Gazzaniga, the trophy is made of solid 18-carat gold

The real trophy is 50.8 cm (20 in) high and weighs 9 kg (20 lb)

World Cup Willie was a lion, inspired by the three lions on the England kit

Replica of the World Cup trophy

MASCOTS FOR MONEY
World Cup Willie was the first World Cup mascot. Designed for the 1966 tournament in England, he represented the increase in commercialism. Since then tournament mascots, such as Footix of France 1998 and Zakumi of South Africa 2010, have appeared on official posters and been sold in many forms.

NEW LOOK CUP
The present World Cup trophy was made for the 1974 Finals in West Germany. Having won for the third time in 1970, Brazil had been allowed to keep the Jules Rimet trophy for good. The new trophy was commissioned by FIFA, despite an offer from Brazil to provide a trophy named after FIFA president, Sir Stanley Rous.

Spanish Football Federation crest

THINKING POSITIVE
In 1978, hosts Argentina inspired their passionate fans with their positive attitude. The star of their winning team was Mario Kempes who played club football in Europe.

ENTHUSIASTIC AMERICA
Despite having no strong tradition of professional football, the USA hosted a successful World Cup Final in 1994. Large and enthusiastic crowds attended all the games. This is a ticket for the game between Italy and Mexico, played at the former RFK Stadium, now the Jack Kent Cooke Stadium, home to American football team the Washington Redskins.

A pack of cards illustrating the stadiums

HARD WORK FOR HOSTS
A country bids to hold the World Cup several years in advance. They try to convince FIFA that they will be able to stage a successful tournament. They have to produce information about all aspects of the tournament, including the stadiums, transport networks, accommodation, and media facilities. Brazil's bid to host the 2014 World Cup finals was successful. The country has hosted the tournament once before, in 1950.

Each ball contains a slip of paper with a team written on it

WHO PLAYS WHO?
Plastic balls like these are used to make the draw for the World Cup Finals. It is a fair way to decide who plays whom. The number of competing teams has steadily increased from 13 in 1930 to 32 in 2010. The present system ensures that every team gets to play three games in the first round. Then, for the rest of the tournament, games are played on a knock-out basis, until only two remain for the grand final.

The balls are brightly coloured for the benefit of TV audiences

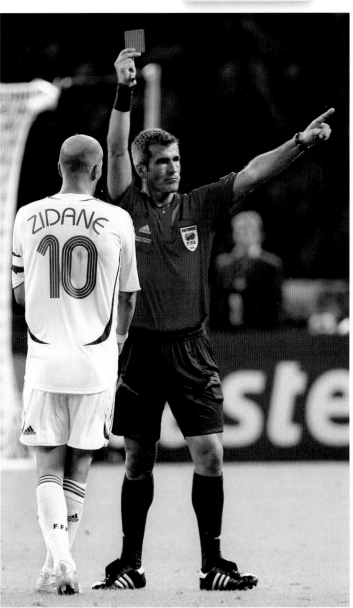

ZIDANE SEES RED
The defining moment of the 2006 World Cup Final came when referee Orazio Elizondo sent off French captain Zinédine Zidane after his infamous head-butt of Italian defender Marco Matarazzi. With the score at 0–0 after extra time, Italy went on to win the game on penalties.

FIRST FOR AFRICA
The distinctive sound of the vuvuzela horn was a feature of the 2010 World Cup in South Africa. Although African teams have competed in the tournament since 1970, South Africa was the first country from the continent to host the competition. The 2022 tournament in Qatar will also break new ground, as it will be the first World Cup to be held in the Middle East.

Cups and trophies

THE MOMENT WHEN a team captain is presented with a trophy and holds it up to the fans is the crowning glory of any campaign. Cups and trophies are the marks of success and the managers of many modern clubs know that, if they are to hold on to their job, their team has to win a competition. For clubs like Real Madrid in Spain, Benfica in Portugal, and Bayern Munich in Germany, finishing as runners-up is considered a failure. The desire to make money has led to the creation of many new competitions in recent years, some of which do not have the same prestige as older tournaments, such as the European Cup or the Copa America.

TEAM TALK
The European Cup was originally for the champions of each country's league. Now the top two clubs compete. The competition was first held in 1956. At the 1985 final at the Heysel Stadium in Brussels, Belgium, 39 people died. A safety wall collapsed as fans of Juventus, Italy and Liverpool, England fought each other.

Programme for the 1985 European Cup final

Corner flags used as decoration

EARLY CUP
This decorative, silver-plated trophy from the 1870s is an example of an early football cup. After the FA Cup was started in 1872, local tournaments for small clubs began to be set up all over England and Scotland along the same lines.

FULL HOUSE
In the 1999 Women's World Cup in the USA, teams played in front of capacity crowds. The final was held in the Rose Bowl in Pasadena, California. Here, US player Cindy Parlow rides a tackle in the final against China. The USA won, to secure their second World Cup victory.

WOMEN'S WORLD CUP
The first Women's World Cup took place in China in 1991. The final was held in Guangzhou, where the USA beat Norway 2–1. The tournament went from strength to strength and the next two events, in 1995 and 1999, drew large crowds. This is the trophy awarded to the USA in 1999.

The gold-plated Women's World Cup trophy has a football at the top

Holding the trophy aloft is a proud moment

PLAYER'S CIGARETTES
ASSOCIATION CUP WINNERS
THE OLD CUP

PLAYER'S CIGARETTES
ASSOCIATION CUP WI
THE PRESENT CU

LITTLE TIN IDOLS
The first FA Cup, on the left, was known as the Little Tin Idol. It was stolen from a shop display in 1895 and was never recovered. The present FA Cup, on the right, was made in Bradford, England, in 1911.

The silver UEFA trophy is decorated with men playing football

Names of previous winners engraved around the base

FROM STRENGTH TO STRENGTH
The Africa Cup of Nations has been held since 1957. Although the first tournament featured only three nations, 16 teams now take part in the competition. Egypt captain Ahmed Hassan is pictured here in 2008 after his team's 1–0 win over Cameroon. This was Egypt's sixth African Nations title.

The Copa America was conceived by Chile, Uruguay, Brazil, and Argentina

COPA AMERICA CUP
First held in 1910, the Copa America is the oldest major international competition. It was originally played for only by South American countries but, in recent years, Mexico and the USA have also taken part. Uruguay won the first official Copa America in 1917 and, along with Argentina, have been the most successful teams over the years. Brazil have not always played their strongest team. Since 1987, the tournament has been held every two years.

SECOND BEST
The UEFA (Union of European Football Associations) Cup was originally known as the Inter City Fairs Cup. The first competition was played over three years, beginning in 1955. Barcelona beat London 8–2 in the two-legged final. When the European Cup Winners' Cup was abolished in 1999, only two European club competitions remained. The strongest sides qualify for the European Cup and the next best play in the UEFA Cup. From 2009/10 the UEFA Cup became known as the Europa League and included a group stage similar to the Champions League.

Playing the game

Two lead "kicking" figures from the early 20th century

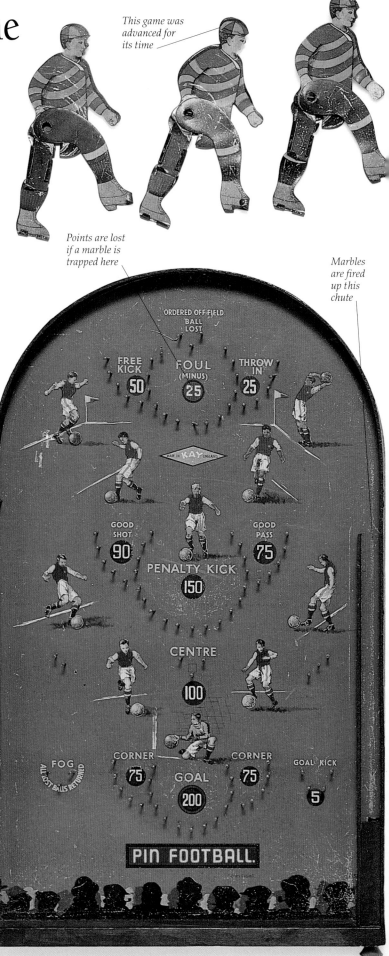

This game was advanced for its time

Points are lost if a marble is trapped here

Marbles are fired up this chute

GENERATIONS OF children have had their first contact with football through toys such as blow football, card games, and Subbuteo. The popularity of football means that, as with other merchandise, there is money to be made from developing new products with a football theme. This drives manufacturers and inventors to come up with a vast range of games based on football, far more than on any other sport. The simplicity of the toys from the past, shown here, contrasts sharply with the speed and excitement of modern computer games. Today, people can experience virtual football games and act out the roles of their favourite players and teams on games consoles.

BALL ROLLING
This hand-held toy was made in the early 20th century. It involves rolling the ball-bearing into one of the small holes.

IN THE TRENCHES
Trench Football was produced for British soldiers fighting in World War I. The player must move a ball-bearing safely past the German generals to score.

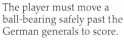

FOOTBALL MATCHBOX
This is the world's smallest football game, probably made in Japan in the 1930s for young children. When the matchbox is opened, a spring is released and the players leap up.

PINBALL
In this bagatelle game from the 1950s, players shoot marbles around the board using a spring in the bottom right-hand corner. Points are scored or lost according to where the marbles stop.

Ball for the Kick game

Downward pressure on one leg causes the other leg to kick

The cards feature different positions and parts of the match

KICK FIGURES
These figures come from a tabletop game called Kick, made in about 1900. A green cloth pitch, and goals with nets are included. Players make the mechanical footballers kick by pressing them down on the table. They are moved around by hand – a feature also used in more modern football toys.

Combination of red and white is a classic football strip

Key fits into the ball to wind it up

SNAP!
This rare pack of snap cards from the early 20th century features football characters. In snap, players aim to collect all the cards. They turn over cards until two identical ones turn up together. The first player to shout "Snap!" takes the pile.

QUICK CHANGE
These wooden blocks, with a different picture on each side, can be jumbled up to make a character. The shin-pads and ball reflect the style at the time the toy was made – 1895.

CLOCKWORK PLAYER
This tin-plate clockwork toy was made in Germany in the early 1950s. When wound up with a key, the figure moves forwards, as if dribbling the ball. The shirt, with its loosely laced neck, is typical of the style of football clothes worn in Europe at that time.

CHAMPIONS!
This game, called Championship Soccer, was made in 1983. It uses two of the classic components of many board games – dice and cards – to govern the movement of the ball around the field. A scoreboard and clock are also included.

Memorabilia

1910 silver Vesta (match holder) advertising the mustard maker Colman's

FOOTBALL appeals to all parts of the community, regardless of age or sex. The game can therefore be used to promote a wide range of items. Football-related advertising and product promotion is not a new phenomenon. In fact, companies were already latching on to the game's popularity in the early part of the 20th century. An understated style and original artwork predominated until the 1950s. This has been largely replaced today by mass-produced items, heavily reliant on star players and wealthy clubs.

Bank Top White Star

Wednesday, now Sheffield Wednesday

Welsh national team

Chadderton, a non-league team

Scottish club, Hearts

BAINES CARDS
These cards, produced in the late 19th and early 20th century, were the forerunners of sticker albums and other collectibles. They featured football and rugby league teams at professional and amateur level and had advertisements on the reverse side.

SPORTS TIN
By the 1930s, original artwork on a sporting theme was often used as a decoration for everyday household items. This tin features football on the lid and other sports, including cricket and hockey, around the outside.

Covered stands are rare in southern Europe

POSTER PAINTING
In this advertising card of the 1920s, an Italian drinks company has illustrated its product in a football scene, instead of putting a football image on the actual bottle.

This label comes from a fruity soft drink. It was marketed as an ideal refreshment for half-time

FIFA logo for Italia '90

SOUVENIRS
Mementos of the World Cup Finals do not stop at programmes and tickets. There is great demand around the world for anything tied to the tournament, such as these erasers from Italia '90.

FOOTBALL FAN
This is a Spanish lady's fan from the mid-20th century, printed in Barcelona. It has a football image on one side and carries a promotional message on the reverse. Many commercial objects of this period were designed to be artistic as well as functional.

HEALTHY KICK
There is no magic ingredient in this drink, but the images would have appealed to football fans. The manufacturers knew that any association with football would improve sales.

This label implies that the drink will promote the robust strength that a footballer enjoys

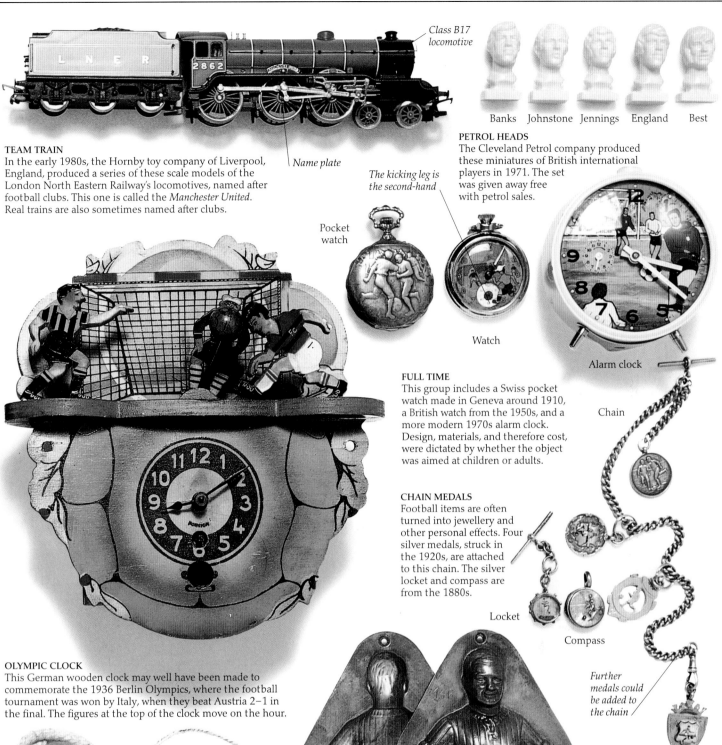

Class B17
locomotive

Banks Johnstone Jennings England Best

TEAM TRAIN
In the early 1980s, the Hornby toy company of Liverpool, England, produced a series of these scale models of the London North Eastern Railway's locomotives, named after football clubs. This one is called the *Manchester United*. Real trains are also sometimes named after clubs.

Name plate

The kicking leg is the second-hand

Pocket watch

Watch

PETROL HEADS
The Cleveland Petrol company produced these miniatures of British international players in 1971. The set was given away free with petrol sales.

Alarm clock

Chain

FULL TIME
This group includes a Swiss pocket watch made in Geneva around 1910, a British watch from the 1950s, and a more modern 1970s alarm clock. Design, materials, and therefore cost, were dictated by whether the object was aimed at children or adults.

CHAIN MEDALS
Football items are often turned into jewellery and other personal effects. Four silver medals, struck in the 1920s, are attached to this chain. The silver locket and compass are from the 1880s.

Locket

Compass

Further medals could be added to the chain

OLYMPIC CLOCK
This German wooden clock may well have been made to commemorate the 1936 Berlin Olympics, where the football tournament was won by Italy, when they beat Austria 2–1 in the final. The figures at the top of the clock move on the hour.

The figure is the same on both halves

SOAP ON A ROPE
The Avon company produced this soap football to mark the 1966 World Cup Final in England.

STRING ALONG
Made in the 1880s, this copper string holder prevents string from getting tangled. The string is pulled through a hole in the top.

CHOCOLATE
Melted chocolate would have been poured into this early 20th-century brass mould and left to cool and set, producing a miniature chocolate footballer with a ball at his feet. This item was made to appeal mainly to children and the general footballing theme would have been enough to make it popular.

The business of football

FOOTBALL IS BIG BUSINESS – fans attend matches in large numbers, club products sell worldwide, and top players and managers earn an incredibly large wage. The clubs and professional players of the 1880s realized the financial possibilities of football but, for many decades, the game carried on at much the same level. It provided cheap entertainment for the paying public and offered a decent living to players and managers. All that has changed now, as club owners and star players stretch football's money-making potential to the limit.

BILLY'S BRIBE
This shirt was worn by Welshman Billy Meredith, the greatest player of his era. As a player for Manchester City, England, he was banned from playing for a year in 1905. He allegedly tried to bribe the Aston Villa captain £10 to lose an important game. This was the first major scandal of British football.

Romário is pictured here playing in Vasco de Gama's white home shirt with trademark diagonal black stripe

The company logo of the club's kit sponsors is displayed in the centre of the shirt

Even shin-pads, worn under the socks, are marked with the name of the manufacturer

GETTING SHIRTY
Replica shirts are a major source of income for professional clubs like England's Manchester United and Spain's Real Madrid. Three or four designs are available at one time and new ones are brought out at regular intervals. Clubs produce hundreds of different products – from calendars to baby clothes; from sweets to bicycles. These can be sold to fans all over the world, reducing the club's reliance on gate receipts.

MANAGEMENT STRESS
Managers are subjected to great stress in the modern game and have to accept that their every decision will be examined by the media. In most of the major leagues, the length of time allowed for a manager to produce a winning team can be measured in months rather than years. In 2007, Brazilian star Romário became player-manager of Vasco da Gama. He scored three times for the club during his stint as manager.

SHIRT ADVERT
Companies have been paying football clubs to put their logos on their shirts since the 1970s. In recent years, Barcelona has been the only major club to buck this trend. However, in 2010 they began a commercial relationship with the country of Qatar, resulting in sponsorship from the Qatar Foundation and Qatar Airlines.

RONALDO'S RECORD

Players today are keen to change clubs regularly because of the signing-on fees they receive. Prices have continued to rocket in recent years, with a new record set in 2009 by Portugal's Christiano Ronaldo. The superstar goalscorer became the most expensive player in football history when he moved from Manchester United to Real Madrid for a staggering fee of £80 million.

Strikers, such as Ronaldo, fetch the highest prices

GROUND FORCE

Advertising in and around football grounds was allowed long before shirt sponsorship. In the 1950s, it featured mainly local firms, but now larger multinational companies exploit the exposure provided by television coverage. Some hoardings rotate, to catch the eye of the watching public and allow more advertisers to use limited space. In some competitions, such as the European Champions' League, the same products are advertised at every match in the tournament.

ALL ABROAD!

Political and legal changes have made it easy for footballers to move abroad and play for foreign clubs. European Union (EU) residents can play in any member state, while players from non-EU countries must meet specified criteria to go abroad. Players from overseas, such as Ivorian midfielder, Yaya Touré, are now in the majority at the Premiership clubs of England.

Ivory Coast's Yaya Touré won the FA Cup in his first season with English side Manchester City

Badge showing AC Milan's club logo

MEDIA MOGULS

AC Milan are one of the many teams with links to big business. Italian media mogul Silvio Berlusconi bought the club at a time when television coverage of the game was increasing. He was able to maximize commercial opportunities and attract star players from abroad.

World Club Cup

EUROPE VERSUS SOUTH AMERICA

The Intercontinental Cup was contested by the top team in Europe and the top team in South America. The first competition was between Real Madrid, Spain, and Penarol, Uruguay, in 1960. Originally a home-and-away fixture won by the team with the highest aggregate score, it was changed to a single fixture in 1980, and was replaced by the World Club Cup in 2005.

The science of football

FOR MANY YEARS, FOOTBALL was not considered a subject of scientific investigation and coaches and players relied largely on knowledge gained from experience. As technology has become more sophisticated, and the difference between winning and losing smaller, ways of using science to improve football have been developed. Nutritionists have transformed footballers' diets, physicists have studied how and why some players can bend the ball, and information technology has made a statistical analysis of the game possible.

BIOLOGICAL DIFFERENCES
For much of the first century of football, women were marginalised on the grounds that they were physically unsuited to the game. However, as the former Brazilian international Milene Domingues shows here, women have all the touch and skills of men, if not the sheer bulk and strength.

ISOTONIC NUTRITION
Footballers can lose up to 3 litres (7 pints) of water during a game so it is imperative that they rehydrate their bodies during and after a match. Isotonic drinks, which contain a small amount of salts and sugars, are the most effective for doing this. The drinks also help replenish the player's stock of calories.

German players exercise their abductor muscles, which lift the leg outwards from the body

Players run round poles to test their capacity to change direction at speed

With one foot off the ground, turning on the run, players develop their sense of balance

TRAINING MUSCLES
Training was once little more than a few laps around the pitch, but today advances in medical science have resulted in highly specialised regimes. Players warm up and warm down to avoid muscle strain and do specific work on individual muscles to help them cope with the range of moves needed during the game.

PHYSICAL DEMANDS

The German national team were put through their paces before the 2006 World Cup, their levels of fitness monitored and recorded in training exercises like this.

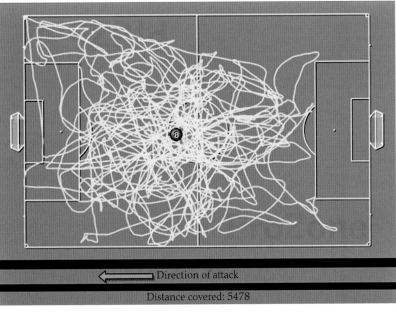

A microchip inside the ball will determine whether the ball crossed the line

A CLEVER LITTLE CHIP

Did all of the ball cross all of the line? It is a question referees, players, and fans are always arguing over. Different forms of goal line technology – including a microchip inserted into a ball stuffed with foam – are currently being trialled in the professional game.

Direction of attack

Distance covered: 5478

PROZONE

Software such as Prozone can track the precise movements of players in a game, recreate passages of play in animated form, and provide incredibly detailed statistics. This screen shows the movements of a central midfielder over one half of a game. The dot in the centre shows the player's average position on the pitch while the distance the player has run is calculated at more than 5 km (3 miles).

FLAGS THAT GO BLEEP

Assistant referees are now equipped with blip flags. If something has been missed, especially incidents off the ball, the assistant can alert the referee by pressing a button on the flag's handle. The referee's receiver, strapped to their arm, will then vibrate or bleep.

Flags with blip buttons like this were first introduced in the late 1990s

The muscles in a player's leg have to learn to switch rapidly from relaxed to contracted and back again

Did you know?

AMAZING FACTS

A three-minute egg

On average, each player in a match has the ball for only three minutes, the time it takes to boil an egg!

In 1965, substitutes were allowed for the first time, but only when a player was injured. Substitutes featured in the World Cup for the first time in 1970.

Luis Chilavert, goalkeeper for Paraguay, rushed out of his goal and scored for his team in a match against Argentina in 1998. The final score was 1–1.

The first person to score from a penalty in a World Cup final was Johan Neeskens for Holland in 1974.

In the 1994 World Cup finals, Russia failed to qualify for the later stages even though they scored more goals in the first stage of the competition than any other team.

The referee for the 1930 World Cup final wore a shirt, tie, jacket and knickerbockers!

John Terry lifting the FA Cup for Chelsea after the 2009 final

Johann Cruyff's mother was a cleaner for the club Ajax in Holland. When she persuaded them to give her 10-year-old son a trial, they signed him as a youth player. He went on to be an international football star.

The goal net only became compulsory in 1892. The crossbar was introduced in 1875.

The first time teams used numbered shirts in an FA Cup final was in 1933. Everton wore numbers 1 to 11, and Manchester City wore numbers 12 to 22.

Eight of the players who won the World Cup for Brazil in 1958 were in the team that retained the World Cup in 1962.

Only eight different countries have been World Cup champions, although there have been 19 finals.

The FA Cup is the oldest competition in football. The highest scoring FA Cup victory was on 15 October 1887, when Preston North End beat Hyde United 26–0 in the first round of the competition. The score was 12–0 at half-time and 25–0 at 90 minutes. The final goal was scored in the five minutes of extra time added by the referee.

Pelé scored 1,283 goals during his senior career.

Half of the world's registered football players are from Asia. Japan's attacking midfielder Shinji Kagawa is one of the leading stars playing in Europe.

Shinji Kagawa

After Brazil beat Italy 4–1 in the 1970 World Cup Final, reporters pursued Pelé into the changing rooms and interviewed him while he had a shower!

Uruguay, with a population of just three million, is the smallest nation to have won the World Cup.

The first international soccer match played by a side with 12 players was in 1952, between France and Northern Ireland. One of the French players was injured and substituted, but after treatment he continued playing, and no one noticed until half-time.

Two pairs of brothers, John and Mel Charles and Len and Ivor Allchurch, played in the Welsh team that beat Northern Ireland 3–2 in 1955. John Charles scored a hat-trick.

QUESTIONS AND ANSWERS

Q Which is the most successful team in international women's football?

A By a very small margin, the USA, which won the first World Cup in 1991 and won it again in 1999. Germany has also won two World Cups (2003, 2007) and hosted it in 2011. However, the USA were also runners up once, in 2011, and have claimed Olympic gold four times – in 1996, 2004, 2008, and 2012.

Q Why was the first World Cup held in Uruguay?

A Uruguay, host nation of the first World Cup in 1930, offered to pay travel expenses for all the teams.

Simone Laudehr of Germany 2011

Q Were old footballs heavier than those used today?

A People make the mistake of thinking that old footballs were heavier than those used today. They were virtually the same weight, but today's footballs have a special coating that stops the leather from absorbing moisture. Before this development footballs could absorb water freely and on wet days the ball could double in weight, often making it as heavy as 1 kg (2.2 lb).

Leather football

Q When were floodlights first used?

A The first recorded use of floodlights was at Bramall Lane, Sheffield, in 1878. The lamps were placed on wooden gantries and were powered by dynamos.

Q When were women banned from playing on the grounds of FA clubs?

A On Boxing Day 1920, more than 53,000 spectators packed into Everton's Goodison Park to watch Dick Kerr Ladies play St Helens Ladies. The FA, worried that the women's game was socially unacceptable, banned women from playing on FA club grounds in 1921. The ban was not lifted until 1970!

Q Which country was the first to be knocked out of a World Cup in a penalty shoot-out?

A Penalty shoot-outs were introduced into the World Cup Finals in 1982 and in the semi-finals West Germany knocked out France.

Q Who plays football in the Olympic Games?

A The national women's football teams compete in the Olympics, but for men it is the national Under-23 teams that take part.

Q Who was England's first black professional footballer?

A Arthur Wharton, originally from the Gold Coast (now Ghana), played for Preston North End as an amateur in the 1880s. He then went on to play as a professional for Rotherham Town, Sheffield United, and Stockport County. He was also a gifted sprinter and could run 100 yards (91 m) in 10 seconds.

Q Why have there been four different FA Cup trophies?

A The first trophy was stolen while on display in a Birmingham sports shop window, after Aston Villa's 1895 victory, so a second trophy, a replica of the first, was made. When Manchester United won the FA Cup in 1909, they made a copy of this trophy for one of their directors. As a result, the FA withdrew this trophy and made a third FA Cup. Due to general damage, this trophy was replaced with a replica in 1991.

Q What has the phrase "back to square one" got to do with football?

A When the BBC first broadcast football live on radio in 1927, the *Radio Times* magazine printed a diagram of the pitch, divided into numbered squares. When the ball was passed back to the goalkeeper, the commentators would say, "Back to square one".

BBC radio microphone

Q When was the first official women's football match?

A Netty Honeyball, secretary of the British Ladies Football Club, organized the first women's football match in 1895.

Record breakers

- Brazil is the only country to have played in the final stages of every World Cup.

- The oldest football club in the world is Sheffield FC. Formed in 1857, the club has always played non-league football.

- Lev Yashin (Russia) is the only goalkeeper who has been chosen as European Footballer of the Year.

- In 1999, Manchester United made history by becoming the first team to win the Treble of the Premier League, the FA Cup, and the European Champions League.

- Real Madrid have won the European Champions League nine times, more than any other team.

- In 1957, Stanley Matthews became the oldest footballer to play for England when he won his 84th international cap at the age of 42. He continued playing league football until he was 50 years old.

Stanley Matthews collector's card

S. MATTHEWS ENGLAND

Who's who?

FOOTBALL IS A GAME OF SPEED and skill, and there are many outstanding players. With international competitions like the FIFA World Cup, extensive media coverage, and a transfer system that allows players to sign for clubs in other countries, footballers from all parts of the world can become household names. Referees can also build up a considerable reputation around the world. These pages contain some of the past and present players who are among the world's best.

Italian referee Pierluigi Collina

GOALKEEPERS

- **SEPP MAIER, WEST GERMANY, B.28.2.44**
The pinnacle of Maier's distinguished career was in 1974, when he won the European Cup with Bayern Munich, followed by the World Cup with West Germany. He played with Bayern Munich for a total of 19 years.

- **PETER SHILTON, ENGLAND, B.18.9.49**
Renowned for his fitness and perfectionism, Shilton made his senior England debut when he was only 20 years old. Over the next 21 years he played for his country 125 times.

- **PETER SCHMEICHEL, DENMARK, B.18.11.63**
Schmeichel moved to Manchester United in 1991, where he won five league titles and two FA Cups. In his trademark "star" save, Schmeichel runs out, spreads his arms and legs wide, and jumps towards the striker.

- **DINO ZOFF, ITALY, B.28.2.42**
Tall and determined, Zoff was almost impossible to beat. He appeared 112 times for Italy between 1968 and 1983 and captained Italy when they won the World Cup in 1982. With club side Juventus he won six Italian League titles and the UEFA Cup.

- **IKER CASILLAS, SPAIN, B.20.5.81**
A lifelong servant of Real Madrid, Casillas made his debut for the Spanish club at the age of 17. An agile shot-stopper, he was captain of Spain for their 2010 World Cup and 2008 and 2012 European Championship successes.

Iker Casillas

DEFENDERS

Paolo Maldini

- **PAOLO MALDINI, ITALY, B.26.6.68**
An attacking full-back and one of the best defenders in the world, Maldini captained AC Milan and Italy, appearing for Italy more than 120 times.

- **MARCEL DESAILLY, FRANCE, B.7.9.68**
Born in Accra, Ghana, Desailly moved to France when he was a child. In 1993 and 1994 he won the Champions Cup twice, first with Marseille, and then with AC Milan. Desailly played a vital role for the French national team when they won the 1998 World Cup and the European Championship in 2000.

- **PAUL BREITNER, WEST GERMANY, B.5.9.51**
An adventurous, skilled left-back at Bayern Munich, Breitner moved forward to midfield on transferring to Real Madrid. He was relaxed and seemingly nerveless in big matches.

- **ROBERTO CARLOS DA SILVA, BRAZIL, B.10.4.73**
A footballer of great skill, with a reputation for taking ferocious free kicks, Roberto Carlos entered the Brazilian national team after the 1994 World Cup. A runner-up in 1998, he won the World Cup in 2002. He joined Real Madrid in 1996, winning the Spanish league in his first season and the UEFA Champions League Final in his second.

- **FERNANDO RUIZ HIERRO, SPAIN, B.23.3.68**
A gifted central defender, Hierro's sure-footed tackling helped Real Madrid to win the UEFA Champions League Finals in both 1998 and 2002.

- **FRANCO BARESI, ITALY, B.8.5.60**
The best sweeper in the world for much of the 1980s and 1990s, Baresi would bring the ball forward and join in attacks. He retired in 1997, having played more than 600 times for club team AC Milan during his 20-year career.

Bobby Moore

- **BOBBY MOORE, ENGLAND, B.12.4.41 – D.24.2.93**
A gifted defender and an excellent captain, Bobby Moore led England to victory in the 1966 World Cup. He played for England 108 times, only missing 10 matches between 1962 and 1972.

- **OSCAR RUGGERI, ARGENTINA, B.26.1.62**
Ruggeri was the heart of the Argentine defence in the 1980s, and a World Cup winner in Mexico in 1986. He captained his national side and won a total of 89 caps.

MIDFIELDERS

• LUIS FILIPE MADEIRA CAEIRO FIGO, PORTUGAL, B.4.11.72
Figo was a European champion at under-16 level in 1989, and a World Youth Cup winner in 1991. He won the Portuguese Cup with Sporting Clube in 1995, and moved to Barcelona, where he captained them to the Spanish league title in 1998, before moving on to play for Real Madrid.

• PAUL GASCOIGNE, ENGLAND, B.27.5.67
An extremely gifted player who possessed excellent ball control and passing skills, Gascoigne's career was hampered by injuries. He was an important member of England's 1990 World Cup team.

• ALAIN GIRESSE, FRANCE, B.2.9.52
A skilful player with excellent technique, Giresse was at the heart of the French midfield at the World Cup finals in 1982 and for the 1984 European Championships.

• FRANK RIJKAARD, HOLLAND, B.30.9.62
Rijkaard made his debut for Holland at the age of 19. A universally admired and versatile footballer, he played midfield for Milan but central defence for Holland. He moved around Europe, playing for clubs in Holland, Portugal, Spain, and Italy.

• FRANCK RIBÉRY, FRANCE, B.7.4.83
The great Zinédine Zidane labelled Franck Ribéry "the jewel of French football" and no wonder. His frightening pace and accurate passing have ensured his place in the Bayern Munich and France teams, as well as the accolade of Germany's Footballer of the Year in 2008.

• ANDRÉS INIESTA, SPAIN, B.11.5.84
A product of the famous Barcelona youth academy, Andrés Iniesta's ability to pass, shoot, and score marks him out as a complete attacking midfielder. One of the most successful players in the modern game, he has won three Champions League titles with Barcelona and two European Championships and one World Cup with Spain.

Franck Ribéry

• SÓCRATES, BRAZIL, B.19.2.54 – D.4.12.2011
A footballer with tremendous balance and poise, Sócrates made excellent passes, but also scored terrific goals. He qualified as a doctor before becoming a footballer, and returned to medicine once his footballing days were over.

• PAUL SCHOLES, ENGLAND, B.16.11.74
Described by the Champions League winning manager Pep Guardiola as "the best midfielder of his generation", Paul Scholes spent his entire career at Manchester United. Famed for his ability to unlock defences with his precise passing and incredible vision, he won 11 Premier League titles and two Champions Leagues during his time at Old Trafford.

Sócrates

FORWARDS

• ROBERTO BAGGIO, ITALY, B.18.2.67
A gifted goalscorer, Baggio helped Juventus win the UEFA Cup in 1993 and the league title in 1995. He was FIFA's World Player of the Year and European Footballer of the Year for 1993.

• GEORGE BEST, NORTHERN IRELAND, B.22.5.46 – D.25.11.2005
An amazingly gifted player, Best had brilliant ball skills and excellent balance. He was European Footballer of the Year in 1968. Many feel that he could have played at the highest level for longer had the success of his club side, Manchester United, continued.

• KENNY DALGLISH, SCOTLAND, B.4.3.51
Dalglish was probably Scotland's greatest-ever player. His ball-control skills were excellent, and he could slice through a defence with his bold, accurate passes.

• THIERRY HENRY, FRANCE, B.17.8.77
A striker possessing terrific ball control, incredible pace, and clinical finishing, Henry was top goalscorer for France when they won the World Cup in 1998.

George Best

• RAUL GONZALEZ BLANCO, SPAIN, B.27.6.77
An extremely gifted footballer with a knack for being in the right place at the right time, Raul scores stunning goals, both with his head and his feet.

• RONALDO LUIS NAZARIO, BRAZIL, B.22.9.76
Ronaldo scored his first goal for Brazil when he was only 16 years of age. An exciting, inspirational striker, his speed and skill enable him to break through almost any defence. Ronaldo was FIFA's World Player of the Year in both 1996 and 1997.

• KARL-HEINZ RUMMENIGGE, WEST GERMANY, B.25.9.55
European Footballer of the Year in 1980 and 1981, Rummenigge was a formidable forward capable of cutting through a team's defence. Between 1976 and 1986 he appeared 95 times for West Germany, scoring 45 goals.

Wayne Rooney

• WAYNE ROONEY, ENGLAND, B.24.10.85
Rooney burst onto the Premier League stage at the age of 16 and starred for England in the 2004 European Championships two years later. Manchester United's powerful forward has already won the Premier League three times and the Champions League in 2008.

• CHRISTIAN VIERI, ITALY, B.12.7.73
A fast, decisive striker, Vieri ended his first season with Madrid in 1998 as the Spanish league's top scorer, with 24 goals. He scored five more for Italy in the 1998 World Cup finals.

World Cup wonders

Since the first World Cup in 1930, the competition has grown in size and stature with a global audience of 715 million people watching the 2006 Final and 32 teams set to participate in 2014. The World Cup's colourful history is packed with super scorers, memorable moments, and amazing anecdotes.

WINNERS

Only seven countries have ever lifted the World Cup trophy:

BRAZIL	1958, 1962, 1970, 1994, 2002	
ITALY	1934, 1938, 1982, 2006	
GERMANY	1954, 1974, 1990	
ARGENTINA	1978, 1986	
URUGUAY	1930, 1950	
ENGLAND	1966	
FRANCE	1998	
SPAIN	2010	

Italy lift the World Cup in 2006

HIGH SCORES

⚽ The highest score in the World Cup Finals was in 1982 when Hungary beat El Salvador 10–1.

⚽ The highest score in a World Cup qualifier came on 11 April 2001 when Australia thrashed American Samoa 31–0.

It's a knockout
During the World Cup finals of 1958, a Brazilian player called Vava scored against the Soviet Union. His team-mates mobbed him with such enthusiasm that he was left unconscious on the pitch and needed medical treatment!

GREATEST GOALSCORERS

RONALDO (BRAZIL)
15 goals   1994–2006

GERD MULLER (WEST GERMANY)
14 goals   1966–1974

MIROSLAV KLOSE (GERMANY)
14 goals   2002–2010

JUST FONTAINE (FRANCE)
13 goals   1958

PELÉ (BRAZIL)
12 goals   1958–1970

JÜRGEN KLINSMANN (GERMANY)
11 goals   1990–1998

SANDOR KOCSIS (HUNGARY)
11 goals   1954

Brazil's Ronaldo

Hat-trick heaven
When Brazil and Poland played in the 1938 World Cup, Brazil's Leônidas da Silva scored a hat-trick followed by a fourth goal. In response, Poland's Ernst Willimowski hammered in three, then another to level the score. Brazil's Romeo finally got the match-winner in extra time.

YOUNGEST PLAYER
Northern Ireland's Norman Whiteside was 17 years old when he played in the 1982 World Cup.

OLDEST PLAYER
Cameroon's Roger Milla was 42 years old when he played in the 1994 World Cup.

FASTEST GOALS
AFTER KICK-OFF

HAKAN SUKUR	(TURKEY) v SOUTH KOREA 2002	11 seconds
VACLAV MASEK	(CZECHOSLOVAKIA) v MEXICO 1962	15 seconds
ERNST LEHNER	(GERMANY) v AUSTRIA 1934	25 seconds
BRYAN ROBSON	(ENGLAND) v FRANCE 1982	28 seconds
BERNARD LACOMBE	(FRANCE) v ITALY 1978	31 seconds

STICKING THE BOOT IN
India withdrew from the World Cup in 1950 in protest at the rule stating that all players must wear boots.

TROPHY TRIVIA

NEW TROPHY

⚽ The existing World Cup trophy was first awarded in 1974. The name and year of every World Cup winner is added to the bottom of the trophy. In 2038, a new trophy will be used because there won't be enough space left for new names on the current one.

⚽ The trophy is made of 18-carat gold! It stands 36 cm (14 in) high and weighs 6 kg (13 lb).

OLD TROPHY

⚽ The original trophy was called the Jules Rimet Trophy in honour of the FIFA president from 1921 to 1954. The Frenchman was a key figure in bringing football to the world stage and setting up the first Finals in 1930.

⚽ The trophy was stolen twice. The first theft was in England in 1966, but a dog called Pickles later discovered it. The trophy was then stolen again in Rio de Janeiro in 1983 and has never been found. It is believed to have been melted down.

GLOBAL AUDIENCE

The World Cup draws one of the largest audiences of any televised event on Earth and is viewed in private homes, public squares and stadiums, and even on mobile phone handsets. The 2010 World Cup in South Africa was broadcast in every single country in the world and the final of the tournament is estimated to have been viewed by an international audience of more than one billion people.

ROYAL REQUEST

At the first World Cup held in Uruguay in 1930, the Romanian team was handpicked by King Carol who organised time off work for the players!

2014 STADIUMS

⚽ The 2014 World Cup will be held at 12 stadiums located all over Brazil, from the city of Manaus in the north of the country to Porto Alegre in the south. The opening match of the tournament will take place at the Arena de Itaquera in the southeastern city of São Paolo, the largest city in Brazil.

⚽ The capacity of the 12 Brazilian stadiums ranges from 41,000 spectators to 79,000. They have an average capacity of 55,333.

⚽ The Estádio Nacional de Brasilia is located in Brasilia, the capital city of the country. Its design is a tribute to Oscar Niemeyer, the Brazilian architect who designed many of Brasilia's most famous buildings. The roof of the stadium is supported by 288 pillars.

⚽ The final of the 2014 World Cup will take place in the Estádio do Maracanã in Rio de Janeiro. One of the most recognizable stadiums in world football, the Maracanã was built for the 1950 World Cup. It is believed to have once held around 200,000 spectators but its current capacity is 78,000.

Estádio do Maracanã, Rio de Janeiro

BLANCO BOUNCE

The 1998 World Cup Finals in France saw the introduction of a new footballing trick, courtesy of the Mexican player Cuauhtémoc Blanco. He broke through the defence by wedging the ball between his feet and jumping.

Footballing nations

THE BEAUTIFUL GAME is played all over the world on streets, pitches, parks, and beaches. In each country, the most gifted players join their national teams to compete in high-profile tournaments. Whether the side has a history of success or no titles to date, fans dream of winning football's top tournament, the World Cup.

ENGLAND

Believed to be the founders of modern football, England and the nation's fans have a long-standing love of the game, with the stand-out moment coming in 1966 when the team won the World Cup.

Football Association founded: 1863
Nicknames: The Three Lions
Top goalscorer: Bobby Charlton 49 (1958–70)
Most appearances: Peter Shilton 125 (1970–90)
Trophies: FIFA World Cup – 1966

FRANCE

With a penchant for attacking football, France are the epitome of entertainment. Although the team did not win an international trophy until 1984, they have made up for lost time by winning the World Cup and European Championship in recent years.

French Federation of Football founded: 1919
Nicknames: Les Bleus (The Blues)
Top goalscorer: Thierry Henry 48 (1997–present)
Most appearances: Lilian Thuram 142 (1994–2008)
Trophies: FIFA World Cup – 1998
UEFA European Championship – 1984, 2000
Olympic gold medal – 1984
FIFA Confederations Cup – 2001, 2003

ARGENTINA

This South American country has a vibrant footballing history with memorable moments, fanatical supporters, and a packed trophy cabinet.

Argentinian Football Association founded: 1891
Nicknames: Albicelestes (White and Sky Blues), Los Gauchos (The Cowboys)
Top goalscorer: Gabriel Batistuta 56 (1991–2002)
Most appearances: Javier Zanetti 135 (1994–present)
Trophies: FIFA World Cup – 1978, 1986
Copa America – 1921, 1925, 1927, 1929, 1937, 1941, 1945, 1946, 1947, 1955, 1957, 1959 (round-robin league tournaments), 1991 (round-robin, then final round of four teams in a mini league), 1993
Olympic gold medal – 2004, 2008

GERMANY

Thanks to great teamwork and skill on the ball, Germany has an unrivalled record for consistency reaching 12 major competitive finals and winning six tournaments.

German Football Association founded: 1900
Nicknames: Die Nationalelf (The National Eleven)
Top goalscorer: Gerd Muller 68 (1966–74)
Most appearances: Lothar Matthaus 150 (1980–2000)
Trophies: FIFA World Cup – 1954, 1974, 1990
UEFA European Championship – 1972, 1980, 1996
Olympic gold medal – 1976

AUSTRALIA

Though Australia dominates in many major sports, football is not one of them. Following years of success in Oceania, the country joined the more competitive Asian Football Confederation in 2006.

Australian Soccer Association founded: 1961
Nicknames: Socceroos
Top goalscorer: Damian Mori 29 (1992–2002)
Most appearances: Alex Tobin 87 (1988–98)
Trophies: Oceania Football Confederation (OFC) Nations Cup – 1980, 1996, 2000, 2004

ITALY

The world's second most successful footballing nation after Brazil, Italy have four World Cups to their name. Solid defensive play and fast counter-attacks are integral to the team's winning ways.

Italian Football Federation founded: 1898
Nicknames: Azzurri (Blues)
Top goalscorer: Luigi Riva 35 (1965–74)
Most appearances: Paolo Maldini 126 (1988–2002)
Trophies: FIFA World Cup – 1934, 1938, 1982, 2006
UEFA European Championship – 1968
Olympic gold medal – 1936

BRAZIL

The most successful footballing nation in history, Brazil has won the World Cup a record-breaking five times with a long line of legendary players.

Brazilian Football Confederation founded: 1914
Nicknames: A Selecao (The Selected), Canarinho (Little Canary)
Top goalscorer: Pelé 77 (1957–71)
Most appearances: Cafu 142 (1990–2006)
Trophies: FIFA World Cup – 1958, 1962, 1970, 1994, 2002
Copa America – 1919, 1922, 1949, 1989, 1997, 1999, 2004, 2007

IVORY COAST

An exciting new prospect in international football, the Ivory Coast reached the World Cup finals in 2006 and many of the nation's homegrown talents now play for great European clubs in their domestic leagues.

Ivory Coast Football Federation founded: 1960
Nicknames: Les Elephants (The Elephants)
Top goalscorer: Didier Drogba 38 (2002–present)
Most appearances: Cyrille Domoraud 51 (1995–2006)
Trophies: Africa Cup of Nations – 1992

DENMARK

Though the nation has produced many quality players, the team has yet to enjoy continued success. The highlight to date was Euro 1992 when Denmark caused a shock by beating West Germany in the final.

Football Association founded: 1889
Top goalscorer: Poul "Tist" Nielsen 52 (1910–25)
Most appearances: Peter Schmeichel 129 (1987–2001)
Trophies: UEFA European Championship – 1992
Confederations Cup – 1995

JAPAN

Football is now the second most popular sport in Japan, following two triumphs in the Asian Cup and a successful co-hosting and encouraging performance in the 2002 World Cup.

Japan Football Association founded: 1921
Nicknames: Nihon Daihyo (Japanese Representatives), Blues
Top goalscorer: Kunishige Kamamoto 74 (1964–77)
Most appearances: Masami Ihara 122 (1988–99)
Trophies: AFC Asian Cup – 1992, 2000, 2004

REPUBLIC OF KOREA

Hopes are high for the Republic of Korea after co-hosting the World Cup finals in 2002. The nation drew international recognition by unexpectedly reaching the semi-finals, knocking out favourites Italy and Spain along the way.

Korea Football Association founded: 1928
Nicknames: Taeguk Warriors, Tigers, Red Devils
Top goalscorer: Cha Bum-Kun 55 (1972–86)
Most appearances: Hong Myung-Bo 135 (1990–2002)
Trophies: AFC Asian Cup – 1956, 1960

MEXICO

A dominant force in the CONCACAF boasting Latin brilliance on the ball, Mexico is rapidly establishing itself as a serious contender in international competitions.

Mexican Football Federation founded: 1927
Top goalscorer: Jared Borgetti 46 (1997–present)
Most appearances: Claudio Suarez (1992–2006)
Trophies: CONCACAF Championship and Gold Cup – 1965, 1971, 1977 (round-robin team tournaments), 1977 (top World Cup qualifying team awarded trophy), 1993, 1996, 1998, 2003
Confederations Cup – 1999

NETHERLANDS

In the 1970s, the Dutch created "Total Football", a system in which every player could play in every position on the pitch. This fluid formation coupled with legendary players has resulted in impressive play but, surprisingly, just one title.

Royal Netherlands Football Association founded: 1889
Nicknames: Clockwork Orange, The Orangemen, Flying Dutchmen
Top goalscorer: Patrick Kluivert 40 (1994–2004)
Most appearances: Edwin van der Sar 130 (1995–present)
Trophies: UEFA European Championship – 1988

PORTUGAL

Under the influential management of Felipe Scolari, Portugal achieved success by reaching the European Championship final in 2004 and the World Cup semi-finals in 2006, but are still yet to win a title.

Portuguese Football Federation founded: 1914
Top goalscorer: Pauleta 47 (1997–2006)
Most appearances: Luis Figo 127 (1991–2006)
Trophies: None

RUSSIA

Although the nation has not won a major title for 50 years, exciting new talents and effective teamwork combine to give Russia a strong basis for future success in international competitions.

Russian Football Union founded: 1912
Top goalscorer: Vladimir Beschastnykh 26 (1992–2003)
Most appearances: Viktor Onopko 109 (1992–2004)
Trophies: (competing as the USSR)
UEFA European Championship – 1960
(competing as Russia) None

SOUTH AFRICA

Following 30 years of exile by FIFA for refusing to field a mixed-race team, South Africa are now going from strength to strength, culminating in 2010 when they become the first African nation to host the World Cup.

South African Football Association founded: 1991
Nicknames: Bafana Bafana (The Boys)
Top goalscorer: Benni McCarthy 31 (1997–present)
Most appearances: Shaun Bartlett 74 (1995–2005)
Trophies: Africa Cup of Nations – 1996

SPAIN

Despite celebrated players and great spirit, the Spanish team have been prone to underachieving in the past. However, they are now realising their potential thanks to success in the 2008 European Championship and the development of rising stars such as Cesc Fabregas.

Royal Spanish Football Federation founded: 1913
Nicknames: La Furia Roja (The Red Fury), La Seleccion (The Selection)
Top goalscorer: Raúl 44 (1996–2006)
Most appearances: Andoni Zubizaretta 126 (1985–98)
Trophies: FIFA World Cup – 2010
UEFA European Championship – 1964, 2008
Olympic gold medal – 1992

URUGUAY

Famous for being the first nation to lift the World Cup in 1930, Uruguay repeated this success 20 years later. These early achievements have been followed by triumphs over the years in the Copa America, but they are yet to capture their former glory in the World Cup.

Uruguay Football Federation founded: 1900
Nicknames: La Celeste (The Sky Blue)
Top goalscorer: Hector Scarone 31 (unknown–1930)
Most appearances: Rodolfo Rodriguez 78 (unknown–1994)
Trophies: FIFA World Cup – 1930, 1950
Copa America – 1916, 1917, 1920, 1923, 1924, 1926, 1935, 1942, 1956, 1959, 1967, 1959, 1967 (round-robin league tournaments), 1983, 1987, 1995
Olympic Games – 1924, 1928

USA

The footballing reputation of the nation that calls the sport "soccer", has improved greatly since they hosted the World Cup in 1994. Qualifying for every World Cup since has shown the critics that the USA is here to stay as a serious competitor.

United States Soccer Federation founded: 1913
Nicknames: The Stars and Stripes, The Red, White, and Blue
Top goalscorer: Landon Donovan 41 (2000–present)
Most appearances: Cobi Jones 164 (1992–2004)
Trophies: CONCACAF Gold Cup – 1991, 2002, 2005, 2007

Find out more

THERE ARE MANY WAYS of getting more involved in the world of football. An important start is to find a club you want to support, and follow their match results. If you are keen to play yourself, you can join a team and take part in a local league. By visiting football museums you will find out about managers, coaches, and scouts as well as players, and will build up a picture of the world of football. The more you learn, the more you will enjoy the football fever surrounding the big competitions, such as the World Cup Finals.

REMEMBER THE MATCH
Match programmes are full of information about the teams that are playing, and are also a great keepsake of an exciting match.

Bob Bishop was the Manchester United scout who discovered George Best, Sammy McIlroy, and many others in the 1960s and 1970s

FOOTBALL SCOUTS
All big clubs have scouts who travel around looking for new talent, whether it be established footballers that the club can buy, or gifted youth players. Outstanding young players will be asked for a trial, and if successful, may be invited to join the club's football academy. Here they receive a general education as well as intensive football training. If all goes well they will work up through the youth and reserve sides to play in the club's first team.

USEFUL WEBSITES

- **To find out about the Football Association:**
  www.thefa.com
- **For information on the World Cup:**
  www.fifa.com
- **For details of the 2014 World Cup Finals:**
  www.fifa.com/worldcup/index.html
- **For information on English football clubs outside the Premier League:** www.football-league.co.uk
- **For up-to-date football information:**
  news.bbc.co.uk/sport/0/football
- **For playing tips and video masterclasses:**
  news.bbc.co.uk/sport1/hi/football/skills

SUPPORT YOUR CLUB
Decide which club you want to support and start following their results. If you can, go to some matches and start your own collection of programmes. Watching the matches and reading the programmes you will soon become an expert on your club's players and management. You will learn about football rules and will have your own ideas on tactics, and how the club should be run. If you get a chance to go to an international match, you will meet football supporters from other parts of the country.

Italian fans cheer their team on

JOIN A TEAM

If you are keen to play the game, then join a school or local youth-club team, and you will quickly find out whether you prefer defence, midfield, attack, or playing in goal. Club coaches will help you master many techniques, such as marking, tackling, dribbling, and passing. Regular training and practice games will ensure you are fit and have the stamina to last the match.

Good close ball control is essential, whether you play in an attacking position or in defence

Places to visit

THE NATIONAL FOOTBALL MUSEUM, URBIS BUILDING, CATHEDRAL GARDENS, MANCHESTER
www.nationalfootballmuseum.com
The world's largest football museum includes the FIFA Museum Collection, and the FA and Football League collections. The museum holds more than 25,000 objects, over 90 minutes of film and sound, and over 1,000 photographs. Interactive galleries allow visitors to measure the speed and accuracy of their penalties, to play table football where all the action is filmed, and to go on a virtual visit to every league ground in the country.

WEMBLEY STADIUM, WEMBLEY, LONDON
www.wembleystadium.com/Wembley-Tours/
A collection that includes memorabilia from England's World Cup victory in 1966.

THE SCOTTISH FOOTBALL MUSEUM, HAMPDEN PARK, GLASGOW
www.scottishfootballmuseum.org.uk
An extensive collection of memorabilia, including film and sound, focusing on football in Scotland.

LIVERPOOL FC MUSEUM, ANFIELD, LIVERPOOL
www.liverpoolfc.com/history/tour-and-museum/home
Displays on the history of Liverpool football club, and its achievements.

ARSENAL FC MUSEUM, HIGHBURY, LONDON
www.arsenal.com/emirates-stadium/arsenal-museum
A collection that highlights the achievements of Arsenal football club over the years.

WEST HAM UNITED MUSEUM, UPTON PARK, LONDON
www.culture24.org.uk/am13521
Displays that chronicle the history of West Ham football club.

THE 2014 FIFA WORLD CUP

In the summer of 2014, the FIFA World Cup Finals will take place in Brazil. This will be the 20th World Cup to be played, and the seventh tournament to be held in a Latin American country. Brazil qualifies automatically as the host nation and another 31 teams from around the world will join them based on the results of qualifier matches. The Brazilian team will be trying to win the competition for the sixth time.

Players still shake hands today as a symbol of good sportsmanship

Captains Billy Wright of England (right) shakes hands with Jean Baratte of France (left) in 1951

Glossary

AFRICA CUP OF NATIONS First won in 1957. African national teams compete for the trophy every two years.

AGENT The person who acts on behalf of a footballer in the arrangement of a transfer or a new contract.

ASSISTANT REFEREES Formerly known as linesmen, one covers each side of the pitch. They signal offside, throw-ins, fouls, and substitutions.

BOOK The referee books players when they have committed an offence. He shows players a yellow card and writes their names in his black book. Players are sent off if they receive two yellow cards in one game.

CAP Originally a hat awarded to those playing an international match. Players count their international appearances in caps.

COACH Runs the training programme, working closely with the manager.

COPA AMERICA CUP First won in 1910. North and South American national teams compete for the trophy every two years.

CORNER KICK Awarded when one of the defending team has put the ball out of play over the goal line.

CROSS A pass made from either wing to a forward at the centre of the pitch.

DEAD-BALL KICK A kick from non-open play, such as a free kick or a corner kick.

A referee's kit

DERBY A "derby match" is a game between two local rival teams.

DIRECT FREE KICK Awarded if a player kicks, trips, pushes, spits, or holds an opponent, or tackles the player rather than the ball. The person taking the free kick can shoot directly at goal.

DIRECTORS The people who serve on a board to help run a club. Some put a lot of personal money into the club.

DRIBBLING Running with the ball while keeping it under close control.

EUROPEAN CUP First won in 1956, it is now known as the Champions League. The top clubs from the league of each European country compete for the trophy every year.

FA CUP First won in 1872. English league and non-league teams compete annually for the trophy.

Using your chest to control the ball

FIFA (FÉDÉRATION INTERNATIONALE DE FOOTBALL ASSOCIATION) Formed in 1904. The world governing body of football, FIFA sets international rules, arbitrates between countries, and runs the World Cup.

FOOTBALL ASSOCIATION Formed in 1863. The national governing body arbitrates between clubs and disciplines players.

FORMATION The arrangement of the players on the pitch. The coach or manager chooses the formation, and may change it during a game in response to the strengths or weaknesses of the opposition.

GIANT KILLER A team that beats a side believed to be of a much higher quality, and from a higher division.

GLOVES Worn by goalkeepers to protect their hands and to help them grip the ball.

GOAL KICK Awarded when the ball goes out of play over the goal line if it was last touched by the attacking team.

GROUND STAFF The people who look after the stadium, the terraces, and the football pitch.

HANDBALL It is an offence to touch the ball with your hands or arms during play.

HEADING A defensive header sends the ball upwards, clearing it as far away as possible. An attacking header sends the ball downwards, hopefully into the goal.

INDIRECT FREE KICK Awarded for dangerous play or for blocking an opponent. The player cannot score directly.

The white ball was introduced in 1951

KICK-OFF The kicking of the ball from the centre point of the field to start the game.

LAWS The 17 Laws of the Game approved by FIFA.

MANAGER The person who picks the team, plans tactics, motivates the players, and decides what to do in training.

MARKING Staying close to an opponent to prevent him from passing, shooting, or receiving the ball.

MASCOT A person, animal, or doll that is considered to bring good luck to a team. Mascots are also part of the increasing commercialization of football.

OFFSIDE When an attacking player receives a ball, two defenders including the goalkeeper have to be between the attacking player and the goal. Players are only penalized for being offside if they interfere with play or gain some advantage by being in that position.

ONE-TWO An attacking player passes the ball to an advanced team-mate, and runs on into a space. The ball is immediately returned, bypassing the defending player.

PENALTY AREA A box that stretches 18 yd (16.5 m) in front of and to either side of the goal.

PENALTY KICK A shot at goal from the penalty spot. Awarded against a team that commits an offence in its own penalty area.

PENALTY SPOT The spot 14 yd (13 m) in front of the goal. The ball is placed here to take a penalty.

PHYSIOTHERAPIST The person who helps players recover from injuries, and who checks players to make sure that they are fit enough for a match.

PITCH The field of play. In the early days the boundaries of the pitch were marked by a series of flags. The FA introduced the pitch markings we know today in 1902.

PROGRAMME Provides information for the fans about the players of their team and of the opposition, as well as a message from the manager.

RATTLE Supporters took rattles into matches until the 1960s, when they started to sing or chant instead. Nowadays rattles are forbidden.

RED CARD The referee holds up a red card to show that a player has to leave the pitch. Serious foul play or two bookable offences results in a red card.

REFEREE The person who has authority for that match to enforce the Laws of the Game.

SCARF Each team has a scarf in its own colours. Fans often wear the scarf or their team's strip when they go to matches.

SCOUT A person employed by a club to look for talented new players.

SET-PIECE Moves practised by a team to take advantage of a dead-ball situation.

SHIN-PADS Pads worn inside socks to protect the lower legs.

SHOOTING A kick towards the goal.

STANDS The areas where the supporters sit or stand around the pitch.

STRIP The shirt, shorts, and socks a team wears. Most clubs have at least two different strips, a home kit and an away kit. A team uses its away kit when there is a conflict of colours.

STUDS Small rounded projections screwed into the sole of a football boot. The referee or assistant referee checks all studs before play starts. Players use longer studs on a wet, muddy pitch.

SUPERSTITIONS Many players are deeply superstitious. For example, they may insist on wearing the same shirt number throughout their career. England footballer Paul Ince would only put his shirt on for a match when running out of the tunnel.

TACKLING Stopping an opponent who has the ball and removing the ball with your feet.

TACTICS Planned actions or movements to gain an advantage over your opponents.

TERRACES Steps where people stood to watch a match before the advent of all-seater stadiums.

THROW-IN A way of restarting play when the ball goes over the touchline. Awarded to the opponent of the player who last touched the ball.

UEFA EUROPA LEAGUE Originally known as the Inter City Fairs Cup. First won in 1958. Changed its name to UEFA Cup and was renamed UEFA Europa League in 2009/10. Some of the best teams from each European country's national league compete for the trophy every year.

A football card

KICKING TO SWERVE THE BALL

PLAYER'S CIGARETTES

World Cup medal

WARM-UP A routine of exercises to warm up all the muscles before the start of a match.

WHISTLE Used by the referee at the beginning and end of a match and to stop play when there is a foul.

WINGER A striker who plays particularly on one side of the pitch or the other.

WOMEN'S WORLD CUP First won in 1991. National women's teams compete for the trophy every four years.

WORLD CUP First won in 1930. National men's teams compete for the trophy every four years.

YELLOW CARD The referee holds up a yellow card to book a player.

The USA Women's football team, 2011

Index

Acknowledgements

Dorling Kindersley would like to thank
Hugh Hornby, Rob Pratten, Lynsey Jones, & Mark Bushell at The National Football Museum for their help and patience; Stewart J. Wild for proofreading; Helen Peters for the index; David Ekholm-JAlbum, Sunita Gahir, David Goldblatt, Susan St. Louis, Lisa Stock, & Bulent Yusuf for the clipart; Neville Graham, Sue Nicholson, & Susan St. Louis for the wallchart.
The publishers would also like to thank the following for their kind permission to reproduce their photographs:
a=above; c=centre; b=below; l=left; r=right; t=top; f=far; n=near

Action Images: 31crb; Toby Melville / Reuters 27cra; Carl Recine 63crb; Bruno Domingos / Reuters 56r; Sporting Images 23c; Sporting Pictures 22c. **Action Plus:** Glyn Kirk 56c; Neil Tingle 10fbr, 60-61 (background), 68b. **Alamy:** wareham.nl 71b; **Colorsport:** 11tr, 21br, 32clb, 39tr, 44-45, 57tr, 68tl; Olympia 35cr, 35tr; Jerome Provost 39bc. **Corbis:** Ben Queenborough / BPI 57bc; BPI / Marc Atkins 60cr; Chen Shaojin / Xinhua Press 17bl; Christian Liewig / Liewig Media Sports 16clb; Frans Lanting 65tc; Matthew Ashton / AMA / Corbis Sports 34tc, 38cl, 60cb, 65cr; S Carmona 44clb; Stephane Reix / Photo & Co. 34tl ; Stephane Reix / Corbis Sports 66-67 (background); Tolga Bozoglu / Epa 62bc ; Universal / TempSport 69br ; Visionhaus 27tr.
Dorling Kindersley: Football Museum, Preston

/ 1974 FIFA TM 48r; Football Museum, Preston / Adidas 18br; Football Museum, Preston / FIFA 46fbr (1998), 49fcr; Football Museum, Preston / Sondico 31ftr; Football Museum, Preston / Umbro 28br; Football Museum, Preston 1, 2bc, 2c, 2cl, 2cla (rubber tube), 2clb, 2fbl, 2fcl, 2ftl (brass pump), 2ftr, 2tc, 2tl (gauged pump), 3c, 3ftl, 3ftr, 4bc, 4bl, 4br (pin), 4cla, 4crb, 4fbl, 4fbr (ball), 4fbr (boot), 4tl, 4tr, 5br, 5fbr, 5ftl, 5ftr (brazil), 5ftr (italy), 5tl, 5tr (dutch), 5tr (hungary), 6b, 6c, 6fcra, 6tr, 7bc, 7cb, 7crb, 7l, 7tr, 8c, 8ca, 8fbr, 8ftl, 8tr, 9br, 9cr, 9fclb, 9l, 9tr, 10cb, 10clb, 10fclb, 10-11, 12br, 12cb (whistle), 12fclb, 12tl, 13br, 13cr, 13ftr (bangladesh), 13ftr (columbia), 13ftr (italy), 13ftr (new zealand), 13ftr (usa), 13tr (australia), 13tr (iceland), 13tr (portugal), 13tr (ussr), 14br, 14ca, 14tl, 15bl, 15cl, 15clb, 15clb (side view), 15cr, 16tl, 17br, 18bl, 18cb, 18cr, 18tl, 18tr, 19bl, 19tl, 20bl, 20tl, 20tr, 21bl, 21cra, 21crb, 21tr, 22cla, 22tl, 22tr, 22-23, 24bc, 24cl, 24crb, 24ftl, 24tr, 25bl, 25cb, 25crb, 25ftl (brass), 25ftl (gauged pump), 25ftr, 25tl (pump), 25tl (rubber), 25tr, 26br, 26cl, 26cr, 26tl, 26tr, 27bc (hammer), 27bc (studs), 27br (nails), 27br (studs), 27c, 27cla, 27fbr (key), 27fbr (studs), 27fbr (wrench), 27tl, 28bl, 28crb, 28tl, 29bl, 29cr, 29tl, 29tr, 30br, 30c, 30cl, 30crb, 30tl, 30tr, 31bc, 31bl, 31clb, 31tc, 31tl, 31tr, 36bc, 36c, 36cb, 36cl, 36clb, 36cra, 36fbr, 36fcl, 36fcrb, 36ftl, 36ftr, 36tr (spoon), 37bl, 37br, 37c, 37clb, 37cr, 37fbl, 37fcrb, 37tr, 38bl, 38br, 38tl, 38-39, 39cr, 39tl, 40b, 40ca, 40cb, 40cl, 40crb, 40ftl, 40ftr, 40tr, 41ca, 41cl, 41clb, 41tr, 42cr, 42tl, 42tr, 43br, 43cra, 43fcr, 43ftr, 43tr, 44ftr, 44tl, 44tr, 45cl, 45t, 46bc (1986), 46bl (1978),

46bl (1982), 46br (1990), 46br (1994), 46c (1954), 46c (1958), 46cl (1938), 46cl (1950), 46clb (1930), 46clb (1934), 46cr (1962), 46cr (1966), 46fcrb (1970), 46fcrb (1974), 46tl, 46tr, 47br, 47tr, 48bl, 48tl, 49ftl, 49tl, 49tr, 50cl, 50tl, 50tr, 51tl, 52br, 52c, 52fbl, 52fcl, 52ftl, 52-53, 53bc, 53bl, 53cla, 53cr, 56tr, 57crb, 61br, 70tc, 71cla; Mark Leech 43bl; The Science Museum, London 61tr. **Dreamstime.com:** Alexander Lebedev 12tr; Greg Da Silva 49br ; Kampee Patisena 20crb; Zedcreations 20crb (iPad);
Getty Images: 62cr, 63tr; AFP Photo / Pierre-Philippe Marcou 58tl; AFP Photo / Roberto Schmidt 50c; AFP Photo DDP / Thomas Lohnes 58b; Allsport 34-35; Allsport / Hulton Archive 34bl; Allsport / Vincent Laforet 50br; Lars Baron / Bongarts 16cl , 63cla; Shaun Botterill 62-63 (background); Shaun Botterill / Getty Images Sport 64-65; Clive Brunskill 14bl; David Cannon / Allsport 33c, 51r; David Cannon / Getty Images Sport 23tl, 64cl; Central Press / Hulton Archive 32cla, 33cr; Tom Dulat 15t; Tony Duffy / Allsport 32br; Mike Hewitt / FIFA 2r; Stuart Franklin / Bongarts 59bc; Gallo Images / Getty Images Sport 51cl; Markus Gilliar - Pool / Bongarts 58-59; Alejandro Gonzalez / Real Madrid 57tl; Scott Heavey 61tl; Patrick Hertzog / AFP 65br; Mike Hewitt 42br; Mike Hewitt / Getty Images Sport 19c; Jasper Juinen / Getty Images Sport 16r; Jeff Vinnick 43tl ; Keystone / Hulton Archive 33bl, 33tl; Ross Kinnaird 58c; David Leah 51cl; John Macdougall / AFP / 2005 FIFA TM 69clb; Josep Lago / AFP 56bl ; Clive Mason 17tl; Damien Meyer / AFP 13l; Paolo Nucci / WireImage 49bl; Doug Pensinger / Getty Images Sport 17c; Popperfoto.com 68cl;

Gary M. Prior 62tr; Bob Thomas 21l; Michael Urban / AFP 36bl; Alexandra Winkler / Reuters 59tr. **Bryan Horsnell:** 42c, 42cl, 42fcl. **Press Association Images:** AP Photo / Lewis Whyld 44cla; Matthew Ashton / Empics Ltd 68-69 (background); Matthew Ashton / Empics Sport 16tr; Jon Buckle / Empics Ltd 70-71 (background); Adam Davy / Empics Sport 62c; Empics Ltd 32tr; Alastair Grant / Associated Press 71tr; Laurence Griffiths / Empics Ltd 69ca, 69tl; Tony Marshall / Empics Sport 28tr; Don Morley / Empics Sport 34tr; PA Archive 34bc; Peter Robinson 63bl; Peter Robinson / Empics 47l; Peter Robinson / Empics Sport 57fcrb; Michael Steele / Empics Sport 41br, 41fclb; Topham Picturepoint 35tl; Witters 35ftr.

Wallchart: Colorsport: cl (biggs), cla (villa). **Corbis:** Franck Seguin / TempSport cb (stadium). **Dorling Kindersley:** Football Museum, Preston / Adidas fbl (shin pads); Football Museum, Preston cr (cards), fcr (ref), ftl (kinnaird), tl (chinese writing), tr (toy); Puma fclb (boot side), fclb (boots sole). **Getty Images:** David Leah / Allsport / FIFA fcrb (world cup); Claudio Villa c (messi).

All other images © Dorling Kindersley
For further information see:
www.dkimages.com